Elevated Resilience

Rising **Strong** through Life's Challenges

COMPILED BY BONNIE WIRTH
Foreword by Michael Bodhi

BIG MOOSE
PUBLISHING

Published by:
Big Moose Publishing
234 Pohorecky Street
Saskatoon, SK S7W 0J3
www.bigmoosepublishing.com

ISBN: 978-1-989840-91-7 (sc)
ISBN: 978-1-989840-92-4 (eb)
Big Moose Publishing 12/2025

This book is dedicated to all the women who came before us—whose shoulders we stand on—whose courage and resilience paved the way for our voices to be heard. Truths that were once muffled and silenced, prayers and sacrifices—lest we forget.

To every woman reading this now, and to the generations yet to come, may your voices be bold, your dreams limitless, and your spirits unbreakable.

We stand upon a legacy, and with each step forward, we honor the past and embrace the future with hope. As we continue to rise— telling stories, raising voices, and planting seeds of change—we carry their strength with us.

Contents

Foreword ix

Intentions xiii

Introduction xxi

Finding Peace 1

Lost Pieces 19

Twelve Steps Home. 45

An Inconvenient Grief 63

Poem: The Worthy Soul. 81

Death Changes 83

Nothing Gold Can Stay 101

Poem: Limitless. 115

Closer to the Heart 117

Pilar and Posporo 135

Well Color Me OK... and Other Acts of Surrender 157

Learning to Trust My Inner Compass. 175

Remembrance: I Am a Temple of Light 191

Elevate Your Life 207

Testimonials for the *Writer from Within* Program 219

MICHAEL BODHI

Michael Bodhi is a bestselling author, teacher, and professional speaker. He has presented to hundreds of thousands of people, teaching wellness strategies in various businesses and organizations that focus on the social, emotional, and career benefits of living more compassionately. His work has also significantly influenced educators and students through an award-winning kindness curriculum used in schools across New England. Additionally, Michael has toured with Louise Hay, Dr. Wayne Dyer, Brian Weiss, M.D., and several other notable authors and speakers.

Michael lives on the coast of Maine, where he continues to write, teach, and develop new programs that ease the pressure of living in today's complex world. You can learn more about his work at michaelbodhi.com.

Foreword

Life can be tough, and for many, that's certainly an understatement. Whether dealing with a traumatic past, grieving a loss, or feeling trapped in an unhealthy relationship, no one is immune to heartbreak and pain. However, as a writer and speaker dedicated to promoting positive mental health, I have seen firsthand how resilient those who face adversity can be—especially women—each refusing to give up and, by some miracle, becoming some of the most courageous and loving people I will ever know.

Women are, of course, the fundamental reason you and I exist. But beyond the miracle of giving life, they also hold the key to sustaining it. Without their natural ability to provide compassionate care, nurture, lead, and make critical decisions, this planet would likely become a barren dust bowl. Additionally, as history has shown, the goddesses of the world possess a resilient spirit unlike any other—the capacity to recover emotionally and physically from hardships that would make most men run and hide in the woods.

The book you're holding proves this point and more. As a collection of essays featuring eleven extraordinary women who have overcome unimaginable obstacles, it not only inspires readers to begin their own healing journeys, but also has the potential to spark a movement. Bonnie Wirth, who brought this project to life through her transformative *Writer from Within* course, embodies the true spirit of the word comeback. As a mother, wife, teacher, leader, and force for good, she is no stranger to dark times. Yet, through the pain and challenges of her life, she not only discovered the light, but became it. Her story is a perfect example that, no matter how difficult the circumstances, suffering can be transformed into service, and each day offers an opportunity to make a meaningful impact on others.

In the weeks before writing the foreword for *Elevated Resilience*, I had the privilege of meeting each of the women who courageously shared their stories here. Saying I've been moved is an understatement. I have cried, laughed out loud, and felt my spirit come alive. But beyond the emotional content in these pages, it is the awe-inspiring vulnerability and strength that each woman displayed—baring their souls—that ultimately becomes an unforgettable gift to you and me, the readers. Furthermore, this book serves as a vital reminder of the bigger picture: that resilient women may be our greatest hope as we navigate a world that feels deeply wounded. In other words, if they can overcome personal struggles with such grit and grace, it seems they hold the secrets to helping humanity do the same.

As a man who has turned to wise women throughout my life to heal my past, I see this book as a precursor to something significant—the start of a revolution where conscious women step into their power and ultimately guide us toward a more emotionally stable world. Because here's the truth: solving humanity's biggest problems will never be achieved through brute force and aggression. What we need now is more love, compassion, empathy, and forgiveness. Men are, of course, fully capable of these qualities. But for me, I trust empowered women—such as those featured in this book—to lead us toward brighter days.

When I was a kid in the 1970s, my sister wore a girl-power-themed T-shirt, which I didn't like much. In fact, I railed against it. Clearly, even as a young boy, my male ego was influenced by societal attitudes. But now, decades later, seeing life from a different angle, the message she displayed on her small frame feels a bit more real: *"Anything boys can do, girls can do better."*

I didn't realize it at the time, but my sister's stance probably prepared me for the message I'm sharing today. (Not to mention the "Elect More Women" sticker displayed on my car). Of course, some will argue that men have advantages in certain areas. But considering the ongoing challenges our planet faces, and after reading this unforgettable book, I am even more convinced that women not only have what it takes to change the world, but they might even be the ones to save it.

Michael Bodhi
November 5th, 2025, Camden, Maine
Author of the international bestseller, *Am I Being Kind: How asking one simple question can change your life and your world*

Intentions

by Bonnie Wirth

My intention for *Elevated Resilience* is to illuminate the profound strength that resides within each of us, and to positively contribute to the collective by promoting and nurturing a world where our shared humanity is experienced more deeply, compassionately, and harmoniously.

I wish that our differences—race, culture, background, and circumstance—ultimately be recognized as surface layers that have concealed the common threads binding us all. May this collection inspire a movement grounded in empathy, hope, and an unwavering belief that when we come together, we can elevate our collective spirit and create a more inclusive and compassionate world.

I believe that the greatest impact we can have is when we recognize that each of us is worthy of love, dignity, and the freedom to be who we are in the world. When I look at the stories of these courageous women, my co-authors in this book, and their diverse voices from around the world, I know it is possible for us to catalyze profound change, creating a world where empathy, understanding, and love become the foundation for our shared future.

May this book be our shared call to rise, reminding us that we can create lasting change—one story, one act of love, one collective heartbeat at a time.

My Intention for the Women of Elevated Resilience

To my co-authors: for you loving, heart-centered women, my intention is that you feel completely seen and deeply valued for the incredible courage it took to step into the purpose of this book—to serve, to lead, and to share your truth. Your journey has brought you here, to this moment, as an author, a leader, a visionary, and a changemaker. The stories you have shared— stories of loss, challenge, and moments of questioning—your vulnerability is a powerful gift to the world. Thank you for the wisdom you offer. Your *Elevated Resilience* will create ripples of healing, hope, and connection that inspire others to find their own voice and truth.

May you stand confidently in the fullness of who you are— embracing everything you've experienced and everything you continue to awaken. May this book, this sacred work of art, serve as a catalyst, propelling your mission forward and deepening your impact. May you be supported, held, and guided as your message touches every corner of the globe, igniting further transformation and awakening in the hearts of many.

You are deeply appreciated, completely seen, profoundly loved and valued. May you always remember the power of your journey, the significance of your voice, and the incredible impact of your presence. You are an essential force in this global awakening, and for that, may you be forever blessed for your presence in this book and the larger community.

My Intention for You, the Reader

Thank you from the bottom of my heart, because I believe that these stories and this book have been made possible because you called—either knowingly or unknowingly—to be a part of this unfolding movement of elevation. Because, in truth, your presence here, your willingness to open your heart to these stories, is a vital part of the evolution of humanity.

My intention for you beautiful souls is that these stories ignite a profound recognition of your own inner strength and infinite potential. As you read the stories of these courageous women, my co-authors from around the world, may you be reminded that meaningful change is possible. May they inspire you to remember that beneath any surface of pain, fear, or doubt lies the enduring truth of your divine essence— that unconditional love and worthiness reside within all of us.

May this book serve as a mirror, reflecting your light and awakening a deeper awareness of your own power. May you feel inspired to step into your truth and be who you are in the world, to unravel what has been holding you back or causing you to play small in the world. We seek to empower you to create a life you will love living.

I encourage you to reach out to the authors, sharing any revelations or insights their stories offered to you or how it relates to your own journey. Community is such an important piece of the healing journey. It is what connects us, supports us, and reminds us that we are not alone.

I would also like to invite you to consider how your own story might serve to uplift and support others—whether through participating in future Elevated collaborations, writing your own book, or speaking your truth. Your story and the experiences that shaped you can be the spark that ignites meaningful change for others.

May you be forever blessed, empowered, and inspired to walk your unique path with courage, grace, and an unwavering belief in the transformative power of the light that is within you.

———•••———

What follows are the heartfelt intentions each author now has for you—tokens of love, light, and hope. Each one, a message to support you on your journey and remind you of your own inner strength.

Mary Driver—I want you to know you are not alone, that you have worth, and you have a voice. Don't be afraid to use it. You have value and a lot to give this world. You are not alone. Peace and contentment are available to you. I want your search for happiness to be over, your sadness to end. I want you to enjoy life and be at peace no matter what is happening to you or around you. I want you to get to know your higher self and learn to trust in the Divine. I want you to never spend another moment worrying again and I want your first reaction to be to trust and know that the Universe has your back. I want you to know life is meant to be joyfully lived. I survived and so can you. Don't get bitter; get better.

Rita Herperger—My intention for the reader is to feel hopeful in the knowledge that no matter their experiences, their level of vulnerability, and their fears, they can find peace and happiness. Learning to live from heart-space is freeing and fulfilling. Learning to live from heart-space allows us to accept our trials without them becoming templates for our life journey. Learning to live from heart-space brings us closer to the divine (whatever that is for you) and fills us with vital life-force energy to live within love, respect, acceptance and kindness for all we meet.

Lori Burris—My intention for the reader is to find kindness, a gentleness with themselves. To be wherever they are and know that everything is exactly perfect in the grand scheme of the Universe, even if you haven't gotten the memo yet. Flying without a map is so underrated.

Buffy Johanson—My intention for the reader is to know we are so much more than we've been led to believe about ourselves. My inward journey of awakening transcends my story and the layers of trauma, conditioning, programming, and limiting beliefs by remembering who I truly am—a temple of light and that that light is in all of us, but is often forgotten—hidden and covered under the layers listed above. You are not broken, and you don't need to be fixed—just remember who you truly are. We are sovereign, diving beings of light that are interconnected with everything. Through this journey, I discovered my mission and passion is to be of service to something greater than myself.

Brenda Gerling—What I want readers to know is that they are worthy and that they matter, regardless of their circumstances. I want them to know that they have everything they need within them and always have. I want them to know that they were born with divine wisdom, and that life can be magical when they bring forth that wisdom from within and allow it to guide their life.

Barrie Tugade—What I want the readers to know is that I said yes before I had the full picture. I said yes to get clear as to where I was going. Saying yes is one thing I am consistent with. Saying yes lights me up in the dark. May all who come across these words recognize the power of their choice to say yes. May you glow so bright you become clear. May you feel illuminated by love with all of your pieces, with all of your parts. May you feel whole because you are. May you remember your name is that of everyone else's. May you remember to say yes to your life.

Carolyn Hampton—My intention for the reader is to share some of my journey to express that our greatest wounds can become our greatest gifts—that we can rise like the phoenix from the ashes and transform not only our own lives, but the lives of those around us. We all have the strength within us to turn our backs on darkness and become a bright light in this world—especially now, when we all need it more than ever. For me, healing my childhood trauma and developing my spiritual gifts not only brought about inner peace, greater self-knowledge, and a spiritual community of like-minded "sisters", it also led me to discover that I have a passion for serving others.

Cathy Morrison—It is my intention to be a beacon of hope to the readers so that they can fully and authentically live. To have love and grief coexist in order to facilitate their transformation and healing. To remember light is always within their reach.

Marianne Lipsius—It is my intention for the readers to know that they are inherently powerful, beautiful, and infinitely valuable, and that their presence in this life matters. It is crucial to know their self-worth and to be their own advocate for the quality of lifestyle that enables them to thrive and glow—the soul-side out.

Patricia Scott—It is my intention to write a compelling story about grief and the nature of love. I hope that my audience will gain insight into the nature of grief—who is allowed to grieve, how we are allowed to grieve, and how to tend lovingly to their own 'inconvenient' griefs.

May the intentions of these words that are offered here be received and may you always remember your right to take up space in the world.

May they serve as a guiding light during challenging times and a gentle reminder of your inherent worth and resilience.

May you carry these blessings with you, to elevate your light and keep on shining!

BONNIE WIRTH

Bonnie Wirth is the visionary behind the Elevated book series—a transformational energetic master coach and mentor, soul entrepreneur, and a leading expert in the fields of mediumship, and trauma recovery. She is the CEO of the Academy of Spirit and Soul, creator of the Aligned Coach Academy™, the Aligned Coach Method™, Aligned Coach Speak™, and Elevated Life.

Bonnie guides individuals to heal emotional wounds, release inherited patterns, and conditioned beliefs. Her work activates inner potential, empowering others to live authentically, purposefully, and fully.

For more information about Bonnie and her work, visit: www.bonniewirth.ca.

Introduction

Authentic Resilience—An Elevated Life

by Bonnie Wirth

Suck it up buttercup, shit happens. Just pull up your big girl panties and get on with it. That happened years ago! It can't possibly still be bothering you.

How many times have you heard something like this or maybe even quietly whispered it to yourself? How often do we tell ourselves that we should just move on, that pain and wounds are things of the past, that we're overreacting and supposed to be "over it" by now?

Or, how when something happens unexpectedly, or we are in the midst of navigating a health crisis, or a difficult breakup, financial stress, or a loved one's passing, we nullify its impact by saying things like, *"Others have it worse," "I shouldn't feel this way,"* or *"I just need to be stronger."* We dismiss our feelings, telling ourselves that we need to "keep it together" or "shake it off," even when deep inside, we're still hurting and processing.

These conditioned paradigms maintain that to be resilient, we must suppress our feelings, silence our voices, and pretend that everything's okay when it's not. It's been deeply ingrained, often becoming an unconscious part of how we cope with adversity and stress.

For eons, women have been led to believe that vulnerability is a weakness, that showing emotion means they are too sensitive, or even "hysterical". Wait! I was one of those women. I kept everything inside—no matter how much it hurt, no matter how frustrated, angry, scared, or upset I was. I hid my true feelings to appear calm, composed, "keep it all together" in front of others, and pretended to be happy even when I wasn't. I kept secrets that were not mine to carry at the expense of my own mental and emotional health.

I played the good girl and martyr who constantly sacrificed her own needs and feelings in the hope of gaining approval or avoiding conflict, all while my sense of self silently eroded. I believed that I was strong, resilient and capable of handling it all on my own. I had convinced myself that I was over my past, even when shadows of those experiences continued to linger beneath the surface. I also thought that to be truly "spiritual", I had to be over it.

I spent half of my life people-pleasing, and trying to pretend that I wasn't carrying any pain. I know firsthand how layered and complex our wounds can be—abandonment, abuse, loss, co-dependency—stories that stack up, one after another, until they feel like part of who we are. The diagnosis of compounded trauma and complex PTSD didn't just tell me what I was experiencing; it revealed how deeply the things I had experienced were running through every fiber of my being. I took my pain and carried it quietly. Was it resilience that caused me to survive? Sure. It is an unconscious, conditioned way in which all humans cope. But surviving isn't thriving. Innate resilience is the bandage that covers up the wounds festering underneath the surface. It blesses us in the moment, offering temporary relief, but it can also prevent us from truly healing.

Here's the thing: true resilience isn't about silencing or ignoring what's alive within us—it's about bravely facing our wounds, listening to what they're trying to invite us towards, and allowing ourselves the grace to truly heal what's been tangled up inside of us. This is what cultivates authentic resilience—a resilience that elevates our life beyond the shallow layers of simply 'getting on with it'—a resilience rooted in acceptance, compassion, and an extraordinary level of self-worth.

It's born from a willingness to lean into discomfort, explore the impact of our experiences, and find understanding on every level—mind, heart, and soul—to create safety in our body. We need to get to a place where our dysregulated nervous systems can find refuge and restore balance.

It's not about pretending or spiritually bypassing where we feel pain, avoiding the uncomfortable truths, or putting on a brave face to mask what's really going on inside. An elevated level of resilience requires us to face everything—the messy, the painful, and the difficult—and to do so with faith in something greater, a purpose or meaning that sustains us.

Finding Purpose from Pain

My co-authors, the women sharing their stories alongside me in this book, are the epitome of authentic resilience. Each one is a shining example of courage and renewal, each one is a reminder that we all carry the power within us to rise. They've faced adversity, experienced heart-wrenching loss, and have endured what tested their very will to live. They've come from hopelessness and despair. They've confronted their own shadows and the dark.

Each one found that writing her story was not an easy process. It wasn't just about finding the courage, or convincing themselves that their story mattered, it was the sheer will of something greater inside of them—something that called them forward to share their experiences and the wisdom they gained along the way. They connected to the writer from within as an act of service. It's been through their writing journey that they've crafted authentic resilience into an elevated state of empowerment, healing, and purpose—showing that even the deepest wounds can become catalysts for growth and meaning.

In embracing their stories, these women discovered that pain, when acknowledged and understood, can serve as a powerful source of transformation. It is often through our most profound struggles that we uncover our true strength and deepen our connection to ourselves and to others. Their stories demonstrate that resilience is not merely bouncing back but rising with intention—using their experiences as a foundation to forge a new path rooted in purpose and compassion. It's here that we discover that we are not isolated and alone, but more united in our human condition than ever before; where we find a collective strength that transcends individual pain, reminding us that we are all interconnected in this beautiful dance of life.

This process of finding purpose from pain is about more than just personal healing; it is about creating a ripple effect that extends beyond the individual. By sharing their truths, the intention of these women is to inspire others to confront their own wounds, to see adversity and pain as a portal for healing, and that their own struggles can be transformed into a source of light for those still navigating their own dark nights. Their journeys serve as a testament to the resilience inherent in every human spirit—a state of elevated resilience that, when harnessed, can lead to an extraordinary life.

The collection of stories included in this book reminds us that all that pain is not the end of the story. It is a chapter—a transformative chapter—where suffering can be rewoven into hope, and loss into new beginnings. It is through the courage to face our deepest fears that we unlock the true potential for growth, purpose, and renewal.

In Service to You—Your Elevation

As you turn the pages of this book, I invite you to take your time with these stories. Allow yourself to breathe deeply into the words that these women courageously share. Let their voices help you remember the light that already resides within you. These stories are more than just words—they're an invitation to awaken your own inner power and to stand renewed in your journey.

They reflect parts of you—the insights, the truths, the depth of your own potential. There is a frequency enmeshed within the pages of this book that vibrates with healing and possibility. Allow this energy to bathe you, uplift you, and inspire you to rise stronger, deeper, and more aligned with your true self.

Trust that as you engage with these stories, you are aligning yourself with a greater awakening of your own inner strength and limitless potential. Let these stories guide you inward, and allow the lessons, perspectives, and truths of these women to open your heart and to know yourself better.

At the end of each chapter, you'll find a beautiful affirmation to further support you. Affirmations can be a powerful tool to reinforce positive beliefs, cultivate inner strength, and deepen your connection to your true self. They can be spoken out loud, posted on sticky notes around the house, or written out as part of your journalling practice. No matter how you choose to use them, do so with intention.

Also included here is what we've coined, 'Your Elevation.' Here, each author shares a heartfelt message or offers to you inspiring steps for you to take to support your ongoing journey. While the first step of any healing journey can often be the most challenging, these small, intentional actions, and messages, can help you move forward on your path. They offer valuable insights, daily practices, and choices that empower you to rise strong through your life's challenges.

These are not just their recommendations; they are lived and experienced expressions and practices that have supported each of them personally towards embodying who they are. By integrating these steps into your own life, and taking their loving messages to heart, you too can actively nurture your authentic resilience and journey toward a deeper, more elevated state of being.

I recommend starting with one practice and giving yourself the opportunity to reap its benefits by applying it consistently for 21 days. It takes 21 days to create new habits of thought and shift limiting behaviors, so allowing yourself this dedicated period will give you the best possible chance to experience meaningful change.

My hope is that these elevation steps become part of your daily life—a sacred ritual to nurture your own authentic resilience. These steps are designed to align mind, body, and spirit—it's about awakening your inner consciousness, holding space for healing, and cultivating resilience rooted in worthiness. Because once you truly embody that worthiness, resilience becomes a life-changing force—fueling your ability to fully live, love, and create the life you truly desire.

The Path of Elevated Resilience

Remember, resilience isn't just about bouncing back or simply enduring—it's about consciously rising into a higher state of awareness, grace, and profound connection to your true self and the universe. When we elevate our resilience, we go beyond surface-level endurance. We move beyond merely surviving and step into a renewed state of being—whole, aligned, rooted body, mind, and spirit—where growth, healing, and transformation are woven into the fabric of our everyday lives.

In our body, it creates a sanctuary, where our nervous system can relax and our triggers subside. It is where nurturing becomes an act of self-love and self-care, a priority.

In our mind, it acts as a powerful anchor that allows us to move beyond limiting beliefs, reduce the chatter of fear and doubt, and cultivate a mindset of confidence, awareness, and inner peace.

At the spiritual level, it reconnects us with our essence—our higher self—the one that is worthy, lovable, and inherently enough, guiding us toward fulfillment and purpose.

This journey—your sacred journey—begins in that space of mindful intention, deep compassion, and unwavering belief in your innate worth. As you move forward, remember that within you resides an infinite capacity to rise stronger, wiser, and more aligned than ever before. The wounds of the past and whatever challenges you may be navigating are not the end of your story but rather the divine invitation to elevate your life, elevate your spirit, and embody the incredible potential of your authentic self.

True resilience is a conscious choice—a willingness to transform pain into purpose, fear into courage, and limitations into limitless possibility. You are the creator of your transformation, and this book is here to guide, inspire, and remind you that the power to elevate your life is already within you—waiting to be awakened and embraced.

Finding Peace

How I Learned to Forgive the Unforgivable

by Bonnie Wirth

At eight years old, I had already begun to despise myself. It's the age when I actually started to hate myself and my life—when I started to believe that I was unworthy and the 'not good-enoughness' set in.

My home life was anything but peaceful; it was incredibly tumultuous, to say the least. Conflict, violence, and abuse were seductive in convincing me that I should never have been born. I felt like a burden to my parents— that I was the reason for their problems and the source of their stress. Perhaps if I hadn't been born, they would be happier. If I didn't exist, maybe life would be easier for my siblings. I felt like my parents' love was not an unlimited resource, and being the youngest of five meant that I must be taking away a lot of the love that was meant for them.

None of this is rational, but in the eyes of an eight-year-old who had witnessed more than any child should in such a short lifetime, it was all I could believe. Compounded by the fact that I had started being molested a couple of years earlier, which coincided with my first suicide attempt, the trauma I was witnessing and experiencing darkened every part of my world. I was already being severely bullied in school too, so I carried this heavy belief that my presence was a source of inconvenience and a constant problem for everyone around me.

There is so much more to the story of my childhood and adolescence that contributed to the complexity of my trauma— that belongs in its own book. Life continued to test my resilience in ways that I could never have imagined. When I was twenty-two, I was faced with a decision that would forever alter my understanding of myself, my faith, and my worth: the decision to terminate my second pregnancy.

I was anxiously waiting in the emergency department at our local hospital, with its stark yellowish-white walls and people milling around, each absorbed in their own struggles and urgent needs. The prognosis for my unborn child was devastating. I had contracted rubella in my first trimester—a contagious virus that can cause severe complications during pregnancy. I never received vaccinations as a child due to extreme allergic sensitivities that made vaccines risky for me, the reactions life threatening. And now, rubella with its risks of miscarriage, stillbirth, and serious, life-threatening congenital disabilities, my doctor's professional recommendation was that I should terminate the pregnancy.

The doctor looked weary, her tired brown eyes reflecting the exhaustion of a long, demanding shift, yet they were filled with genuine compassion as she began explaining the situation.

As I sat there, listening to her, almost devoid of emotion, she confirmed that what I had been dealing with the week earlier was indeed rubella. She also confirmed the fact that I was seven weeks pregnant. She went on to explain that the baby's health was at grave risk as was my own as the virus was still in my system. I needed an abortion as soon as possible to avoid further complications.

The instant the word "abortion" came out of her mouth, the nurse quickly grabbed her arm, pulled her aside and not-so-quietly explained to her that this was not a conversation we could have freely since it was a Catholic hospital. The doctor immediately turned to me before the nurse even had the chance to finish explaining the hospital's policies. Cutting her off midsentence, the doctor asked me to meet her at her office in a half hour where we could talk privately.

I left the hospital triage room in complete shock; my head spinning as I tried to digest the decision that was in front of me, the reality of the situation pressed in. Nolan was at work, so I drove straight to the grocery store where I found him alone in the aisle stocking shelves. As soon as he saw me, he knew it wasn't good news. We leaned against the shelf instead of each other not wanting to make a public spectacle of things. He was as shocked as I was, lost for words and grappling with the news. I only had a few minutes to bring him up to speed before I hurried off to the doctor's office. As I left, he gave me a quick hug, reassured me that he loved me, and that things were going to be okay.

We lived in a small town, so the drive from the grocery to the doctor's office took less than five minutes, but it was the most agonizing five minutes of my life, each second dragging on as I braced myself for the painful appointment and the weight of the fears I couldn't escape. There was both a moral and spiritual conflict stirring within me. I had always been pro-life. I was Catholic. I was holding on to the belief this wasn't just a fetus, but that life was sacred upon conception. The mere fact that I was even contemplating the abortion felt like the worst sin—a violation of God's law. How could I ever be forgiven? How could I reconcile my faith with the reality I faced? The guilt tore at me.

My appointment with the doctor went as well as could be expected. She outlined that due to the virus, the fetus' development was already compromised. She explained the intricacies of what this meant, and how continuing the pregnancy could lead to irreversible suffering for my unborn child, or even death for both of us. She also encouraged me to consider the son I already had, and what either of these scenarios would mean for him. It wasn't an attempt to manipulate my decision; instead, she was gently guiding me to confront the reality of the situation and think beyond my own beliefs—reminding me that my choices had far-reaching consequences, not only for myself but for the life I already carried.

The inner turmoil combined with what she so matter-of-factly outlined made the decision feel almost impossible. I burst into tears. She reached over and placed her hand softly on mine and said, *"Bonnie, you are so young. This doesn't mean you cannot have another baby in the future. But to carry the responsibility of what bringing this baby into the world will mean for you and for your family, if either of you survive, is not something any of you deserve."* I looked at her, wiping my tears with the back of my hand. Slowly nodding my head, the words almost choking me, I said, *"Okay. Go ahead and make the appointment."*

Three days later, Nolan and I found ourselves at the city hospital.

The hour and a half drive there was heavy with silence—neither of us spoke much, only exchanging a few words here and there. *"Do we have everything? Yes."*, *"Do you need anything? No, do you? No."*, *"What time do we need to be there again? 8:00 a.m."*, *"What time do I need to pick you up? The hospital will call you."* He stayed at the hospital with me until I was called into the day surgery ward. We simply looked at each other; our eyes filled with the unspoken. We muffled our whispered "I love you's" and our goodbyes. I followed the nurse down the hall; the walls seemed to close in around me. Nolan went the other way, to wait helplessly in the quiet, knowing he wouldn't be able to protect me from what lay ahead but unable to do anything else.

I put on the hospital gown the nurse handed to me and walked with her into the day surgery room where I was shown to a bed—my place of refuge before and after the D&C. Tears welled up as the anesthesiologist asked me to count back from ten. When I woke up, slowly regaining consciousness and trembling, the nurse was there, gently caring for me. I was still crying, feeling raw and overwhelmed by the weight of what I had just done. She said, *'Oh good, you're awake. You were out a little longer than we expected. You must have needed the rest. I'll call Nolan and let him know he can come get you."*

An hour later I was back in my street clothes and walked into the waiting room expecting to see Nolan, but he hadn't arrived. Still not feeling well from the anesthetic, emotionally depleted, numb and scared to grieve for my unborn baby, I sat down to wait. I wasn't even aware of time passing until he walked through the door three hours later. I had no strength to say hello. He rushed over to me apologizing. He had been on his way to pick me up when he was t-boned driving through the intersection. The other driver had run a red light totaling our car. He was shaken up considering everything, but was not hurt, at least not physically. Fear shattered my numbness as I realized I might have lost the man I had hoped to marry, along with my unborn child, all on this same devastating day. I could barely breathe, let alone hear him explain the game plan as we left the hospital, other than his Uncle Mike—now our chauffeur—was there to drive us home.

After that, everything became pretty much a blur. I convinced myself I had to be strong. Besides, I had this beautiful little boy waiting at home who needed me to be okay—so I pushed aside my grief. I rationalized that other women had gone through worse, and somehow, I would find a way to seek God's forgiveness. I only confided in my sisters about what happened, though I'm sure Nolan's mom likely pieced it together, especially since she cared for our son while we were away. When she asked what kind of procedure I had, I told her it was a D&C. She went quiet for a moment, then simply nodded. She understood more than I was willing to say.

I remember one of my sisters calling me a few weeks after the abortion. She excitedly shared how she had a dream the night before—how my little girl had come to her and shown her how happy she was, playing with the other children in Heaven. She told me that my daughter wanted me to know she was okay, and that what I had done was alright—that I needed to forgive myself.

But instead of bringing me peace, even though I was grateful to my sister for sharing, her message only angered me. It intensified my longing for my unborn baby because I so desperately wanted to be the one to talk to her. I wanted to feel her presence, to experience her spirit firsthand, just as I had with so many other people's loved ones throughout my life. It made me resent my gift as a medium. I hated myself for not being able to form a relationship with her in the afterlife. I was positive it was because she hated me too. And I was jealous—resentful that my sister had this experience with my daughter, and I hadn't. It crushed me.

As time went on, my grief transformed into shame—an unbearable weight that seeped into every part of my mind and heart. It was a quiet, relentless presence, whispering at the edges of my consciousness, filling me with a deep sense of failure as a mother, as a Catholic and this unworthiness that I just couldn't shake. It only fed into my deep self-hatred. It made me question everything—my choices, my values, my heart—where every mistake was proof of my inadequacy. I felt like I had betrayed God and everyone I loved, including my unborn baby. That no matter how hard I tried, I would never find peace with what I had done.

The doctor was right. Eventually, I did have two more kids—a girl and another boy—making me a mother of three; however, I never got over my unborn baby. I never forgot that I was a mother of four. Especially every Mother's Day. The day was always tinged with sadness, even though I was surrounded by love. On one hand, I was being celebrated by these three amazing little humans I was lucky enough to call my own, and on the other, the absence of my unborn baby was still raw. I longed for the child that I never had the chance to hold. I never had the chance to watch this baby grow. I knew this baby was a girl because of what I knew deep down inside, and my sister confirmed it. I always wondered what she would have looked like, and what the sound of her laughter would have been. At the same time, my guilt and shame made me believe that I didn't have a right to mourn this little one, because I was the one who made the decision to "kill" her.

Hating myself because of my abortion was an understatement. I didn't like who I saw in the mirror—this heavy weight of despair and self-loathing that diffused into every thought, every breath, every cell. The trauma of my past mixed with the choice I made that one day long ago, was growing more toxic within me.

Then one night, I was awakened by what I can only describe as an extraordinary sight. There was this beautiful little girl standing beside my bed, her presence so delicate. She had this big smile and long, flowing blonde hair that seemed to be shimmering—this little emanation of love, right there beside me. Then I heard her sweet voice. "*Mommy,*" she whispered, "*it's alright. You haven't lost me. I am still your baby girl, and I will always be part of the family.*" Her words flowed like a balm to my shattered soul. She reached out with a tenderness that quelled my guilt—she was unbroken by the choice I had made.

"*I am not sad, and nor do I hate you,*" she continued softly. "*It was me who asked you to end that pregnancy. I changed my mind, Mommy. I didn't need the life experience to learn my lesson about love. In fact, from here, I can be that love—for you, for Daddy, for my brothers and my little sister, who by the way, looks exactly like me. You only need to look at her to imagine what I would have looked like. Oh, and I would have giggled just like you too. Forgive me for leaving you, Mommy. Forgive me for asking you to do what you did.*"

What? My sweet baby girl (which has become her name since that day) had asked me to forgive her? Of course I would. When it came to my kids, that part was always the easiest—because, as their mom, it was easier to love them than it was to love myself. But what also jolted into my awareness was that she had asked me to forgive myself all those years ago too. And I hadn't. Instead, I had carried my guilt and shame in silence, refusing to let go, afraid that forgiving myself would mean I was letting her go, and me off the hook.

I'm not really sure if this was the exact moment my healing journey began—I can't recall one defining moment where I could say, "*Right there—that's when it started.*" Because, at that point in my life, my past and present were colliding on so many levels. But I do believe it became a portal for my healing; a chance to finally begin to take a few steps forward from my past. The chance to start forgiving myself for the first time. It was like a permission slip I didn't even know I was waiting for.

And in order to do that, I knew I needed to begin loving myself, because I understood that hate and forgiveness cannot coexist. That much I knew from Christ's teachings. I couldn't make room for true forgiveness if I was still holding on to the self-condemnation that shame had taught me. I had to start treating myself with kindness, patience, and compassion—learning to love myself more, not less. I realized that healing required me to let go of the harsh judgment I had carried for so long and to nurture a new inner voice rooted in acceptance and love—none of which was an easy process.

But based on what I was taught, forgiveness also felt like an impossible feat—this arduous process of needing to repent and grovel at God's feet for redemption. Only when God deemed you worthy after you jumped through a few hoops and scoured your soul, only then could you be forgiven. It was a concept that placed forgiveness far outside of my control, conditional upon the Big Guy in Heaven rather than my own willingness to forgive myself. By this point in my life, I had already stepped away from Catholicism and had converted to Lutheran—another step on my journey to know my truth better. Although many of the core beliefs between these two religions were aligned, my Catholic upbringing was still very ingrained in me, shaping my understanding of sin, grace, and forgiveness. That sense of needing to earn forgiveness, to prove my worthiness, lingered in my subconscious, making self-forgiveness feel almost like an impossible, unreachable goal. Because as I shared at the beginning of this story, I had already believed that I was unworthy of it. Unworthy of love, of forgiveness, of grace, of mercy—you name it, and it felt like I had it withheld from me, like a withheld blessing I could never access.

I considered all these layers of pain, guilt, and longing—each one intertwined with my deepest fears and unspoken truths—maybe this is where my healing journey began? The realization that I needed to allow myself space to feel and observe what was unfolding within me, without rushing to find answers or quick fixes meant that I needed help. And I also didn't know how to really forgive myself and deal with everything else that was coming up at the same time. I needed help with that too. I could not do it alone. Exploring what it truly meant to face the pain of my past and sit and breathe without pushing it away was a process I would have rather run away from if left to my own devices.

When it came to spiritual matters, I did what seemed to be the most logical first step: I tried speaking with my pastor. But the problem was that I could never admit to him that I was a medium. The church refuted such beliefs and considered them incompatible with my faith. Which meant I couldn't share with him about my experience with my daughter's spirit. Or that she asked me to forgive myself and that I needed help to do it for her. I felt trapped between what I instinctively knew to be true about myself and the rigid doctrines that told me I was wrong, dangerous even. It was a barrier with him that I couldn't cross.

Perhaps a psychologist could help? I found this woman, who was truly wonderful. She was easy to open up to. She helped me begin to make sense of the impact of trauma on my mind and heart, gently guiding me through the tangled web of pain and guilt I had carried from my abortion. Her presence offered a new space—safe and supportive—where I could begin to explore the darker parts of my story without shame. That was until I shared the message my sister had given me as well as my own encounter with my sweet baby girl's spirit. She felt medication would be helpful to manage my delusions. I never went back.

Several years later a friend of mine recommended that I go see a medium who lived in a nearby community. She had just had a reading and was blown away by the experience. She wasn't aware of anything I had been dealing with, or the fact that I, too, was a medium—I was still in the closet with all of it. But I took her advice and quickly made an appointment.

Maybe this was actually when my healing journey started? But as I said, there were a lot of moments that could be defined as that phenomenal turning point in my life. After my first reading with her, and through several more that followed, I not only started to understand myself better, but through the messages I was receiving from my angels, I was introduced to what true, genuine forgiveness really was—an allowing of unconditional love.

My angels guided me towards self-love practices as a starting point on my path to forgiveness—as a starting point to loving myself, my past, my decisions, and others through the eyes of the Divine. They explained I needed to fill my cup with what I longed for— love, respect, compassion—to the point that it would overflow. And from this state of overflow, there would be a softening where forgiving myself would then become easier.

I was also guided to use the following six affirmations as my daily affirmative prayer and forgo the prayers, at least for now, that I had practiced through the church until I could sort out what was true for me.

1. I Am Infinite Love.
2. Forgiveness Is My Inherent Birthright.
3. I Am of Divine Magnificence.
4. I Am the Perfection of God Itself Made Manifest.
5. I Am Worthy Beyond Measure.
6. I Am Loved Unconditionally.

Hearing the statements spoken out loud to me in that session was one thing. But gradually, as I repeated them daily and let their truth sink in, I began to feel a subtle shift. These powerful words started to gently unravel the unworthiness and self-hatred that had long been rooted inside of me.

During another session with her, I was introduced to the *Teachings of Abraham,* by Esther and Jerry Hicks, which center around the power of our thoughts and beliefs in manifesting our reality. These teachings emphasize that our feelings are guidance, and that aligning with positive vibrations can attract the life we desire. I was beginning to understand that I held the power to shape my experiences and co-create my life with the Universe, and All That Is—Infinite Love, Infinite Truth, Infinite Source.

In another session, I was introduced to *A Course in Miracles,* which emphasizes forgiveness, inner peace, and the idea that love is our true nature. It teaches that miracles happen when we let go of fear and judgments and reconnect with our divine essence. These teachings illuminated another perspective of Christ's teachings, the importance of compassion, both for me and others. It helped me to begin to look for the divine within every situation and person and to ultimately, begin to seek what was holy and divine within myself.

Each of these books and their teachings began to light me up. They awakened a deep sense of hope and possibility within me, igniting a realization that I was more than my past beliefs or limitations. It felt as if my heart had already grown two sizes, just like the Grinch. My soul was stirring, and I was finally remembering that greater truth inside of me.

But I still hadn't mastered self-forgiveness. Even though I was doing all 'the things'—engaging in affirmations, practicing gratitude, indulging in these inspiring teachings, and surrounding myself with positive energy—I hadn't fully let go of the judgments I held against myself. It was as if I was diligently working on my inner growth, yet there was still a lingering sense of shame and self-criticism that was running through my system.

I was no longer attending church. Instead, I began to study Buddhism, not in depth, but in a more accessible and intuitive way, seeking principles that could support my healing and growth. I was drawn to teachings on mindfulness, compassion, and the impermanent nature of all things. These concepts helped me to understand that suffering is part of life, and that I had the power within me to transform my relationship with pain through acceptance.

More importantly, it led me to a deeper understanding of forgiveness—both for myself and others. Buddhism taught me that holding onto anger and guilt only prolongs suffering, whereas true forgiveness involves releasing attachment to past hurts and recognizing the inherent goodness and impermanence of all beings. It helped me see that forgiving myself was about freeing myself from the chains of shame and regret. Through these teachings, I learned that forgiveness is a gift I am giving myself. Not something that I had to give others—something I could give to me, for my peace, for my healing, and for the space to move forward with a lighter heart.

I began incorporating the three directions of forgiveness into my meditation practice—something I was inspired to do by Jack Kornfield, a renowned Buddhist teacher and author whose teachings on loving-kindness and compassion have deeply influenced my spiritual journey. It's a practice I still actively do to this day.

1. I ask for forgiveness from those I have harmed by acknowledging my mistakes and the ways I have hurt, harmed, or betrayed others, both knowingly and unknowingly. For the ways I have hurt them, I ask for their forgiveness.

2. I forgive myself for the ways I've caused myself suffering, by hurting, betraying, or abandoning myself. I offer myself forgiveness with mercy and compassion. For the ways I have hurt myself, I forgive myself.

3. I offer forgiveness to others who have hurt me. To those that have hurt, harmed, betrayed, or abandoned me, both knowingly and unknowingly. To the extent that I am ready, I offer you forgiveness. I forgive you.

I combined this approach with directing energy intentionally from my heart outwards on my inhale, and inwards on my exhale, like a breath of light that is giving and receiving forgiveness as I recite each of these prayerful statements. I believe this practice is what really supported me to unravel what had been locked inside—what had been holding me back from loving myself and my life. I've shifted.

My faith is greater than any one doctrine, my worthiness restored, and my understanding of the power of our choices has deepened. I believe we hold the power to shape our destiny through the choices we make. I've come to fully embrace pro-choice and to honor all women—including myself—to make decisions about our own lives and bodies. I truly believe that these choices are fundamental to our dignity and sovereignty—we all have the right to determine her own path.

I've come a long way, and I hardly recognize the woman I used to be. Yet, I hold a deep compassion for her—that previous version of me—for all she endured and the struggles she faced. I love who I was before I knew I was truly worthy. I no longer feel ashamed of my choice that day, nor do I hate myself or my life. At the request of my sweet baby girl, I have finally let go of the shame and self-judgment that weighed down so heavily on me since that one fractured day. I have forgiven myself and it's honestly been the most liberating gift I could ever have received.

It doesn't mean that I no longer yearn for what could have been. I do. I still wonder what life might have been like with her here. What it does mean however is that I have found a sense of peace. Isn't that what healing is really about—the ability to accept our past with grace and find the love inside to move forward? Maybe, just maybe, this is where my journey begins?

I've come to understand that it's impossible to simply think ourselves out of hurting, or to ignore what's happened. Because what happened doesn't just stay in our minds—it's embedded in our emotions, it's encoded in our energy, and it lives in every part of our essence. Our wounds affect us on a fundamental, energetic level— our thoughts, our feelings, our physical bodies, and even our soul.

For so long, I believed that if I just pushed harder, distracted myself enough, or stayed busy, I could somehow outrun this pain. But ignoring it was only adding more layers of disconnection. Pretending nothing was wrong only deepened the wounds. It took me years of effort—learning to face those feelings, sit with the discomfort, and slowly peel back the layers of pain—to realize that healing isn't about fixing or erasing what's happened. It's about accepting the reality of our wounds, understanding their impact, and choosing to rewrite the story with compassion, love, and a willingness to do the deeper work. Healing happens when we stop simply surviving and start choosing to explore what lies beneath the surface—from surviving to thriving, from masking to authentic resilience.

And here's the thing—living a disingenuous existence, pretending everything's fine when it's not, can keep us from forming deep, meaningful connections. It can impact our relationships on a fundamental level, fueling feelings of unworthiness and making us feel invisible or undeserving of love and support. When we can't or won't articulate our truth, we stay stuck in the silence, and that silence keeps us from truly healing.

I know this all too well—my abortion was a secret, and I carried the burden of those intense dark feelings alone for a long time. I was conditioned from a young age to suffer in silence, to hide what was really going on inside, to keep family secrets, and to try to fix myself without ever truly opening up. I can look to the generations of women in my own family to see how this cycle repeats itself: avoidance, shame, and emotional disconnection. Avoidance gets us nowhere—except perhaps deeper into regret. It's by breaking this cycle—by opening up, accepting our feelings, and seeking support—that we can begin to heal and create a different future for ourselves and the women yet to come.

Healing begins when we stop hiding and start telling our truth to ourselves and to others no matter how uncomfortable. Because genuine connection and authentic resilience are born from recognizing that we're not alone in this life, and that our wounds don't define us—they are merely part of the story we're here to rewrite.

My Affirmation

In addition to the ones that I shared in this chapter, simply, "I Am".

Your Elevation

I encourage you to consider actively engaging with the 3 directions of forgiveness that I highlighted.

A 'Ritual of Release' is another powerful way to let go and allow forgiveness into your heart. The act of writing down your regrets, mistakes, feeling of guilt or shame allows you to confront and acknowledge what's inside of you more consciously.

Write it all down, don't censor a thing—I forgive myself for

_____.

Next, recite out loud, "It is my intention to forgive myself for what is written on this piece of paper. Thank you. It Is Done, and So It Is." Then run the paper through a shredder, cut it up with scissors, or carefully burn it.

Upon completion, put your hand on your heart, and recite an affirmation that supports and nurtures you.

MARY DRIVER

Mary Driver, in her mid-60s, is a passionate woman and proud mother of four daughters, three stepchildren, and grandmother to 11 grandchildren. After earning a Business Administration certification, she worked in radio promotions, media sales, fitness coaching, chakradancing, creatively fit coaching, and finance management at an RV dealership. Now retired, she lives a creative and adventurous life, enjoying art, sewing, reading, and outdoor activities like skiing, paddle boarding, hiking, cycling, golf, fishing, and RVing—drawing her closer to nature. A lifelong learner, Mary constantly takes courses in self-improvement and personal growth. Her curiosity sometimes leads to taking on too much, but her energy and enthusiasm keep her inspired. With more ideas than time, she continues to motivate others with her creativity, positivity, and zest for life.

Email: m.driver@live.com

Lost Pieces

A Journey to Wholeness

by Mary Driver

My story begins with what I lost: family, innocence, and my child and ends with what I found: strength, compassion, and wholeness. Some losses leave scars that never fully fade, but they also carve out space for unexpected miracles and new beginnings. I discovered a light within me that refused to be extinguished. This is the story of how I found hope, even when all seemed lost.

———•◦•———

I was awakened abruptly by a sudden jab of pain that shocked and paralyzed me. My body felt frozen, and fear surged through me as I tried to make sense of what was happening. Lying beside me, my 22-year-old boyfriend stirred, still groggy from sleep. He blinked and looked over at me, confusion evident on his face, and asked what was going on. The intensity of the pain made it difficult for me to respond, as he tried to understand the situation.

It was early in the morning on New Year's Day 1978, and the moment had arrived. My baby was ready to be born—now! Although he or she was not due for another two weeks, the urgency could not be denied; my child was eager to enter a world that was not ready for such an early arrival. Especially, my own world—one that belonged to a girl barely 16, completely unprepared for what was about to unfold.

As I breathed through the pain, it became clear how little I was prepared for this experience. I had not attended any prenatal classes or received any formal education on childbirth. I struggled to maintain control over my body and emotions, relying on instinct and sheer determination to get through each wave of pain.

The fear that washed over me was almost unbearable, yet it was a familiar feeling I had encountered many times before. I understood, even in the midst of panic, that this was something I simply had to face. The next few hours unfolded in a haze, details slipping away as the intensity of the moment took over.

One memory stands out with striking clarity. While I was being wheeled into the delivery room, a powerful realization struck me: No one else could do this for me. No matter how much help was offered, this was a journey I had to make entirely on my own. The sense of isolation was profound; the task ahead could not be handed off or shared. In that moment, I understood fully that the responsibility—and the strength required—rested solely with me.

Thankfully, just a few hours later, my beautiful baby girl, weighing just over six pounds, came into the world. The nurse, her face glowing with joy, held her up for me to see. In that instant, I turned my head away, unable to allow myself to look at her. Deep down, I knew that if I did—if I allowed myself to truly see her—I would not be able to go through with the adoption process. The pain of separation loomed larger than any physical discomfort I felt.

After the delivery, I endured several stitches, but they did nothing to mend the immense wound in my heart. The emotional pain was overwhelming and far exceeded the physical pain I was experiencing. It was a wound that would remain open for years, draining my life and vitality, leaving me feeling hollow and lost.

There are only a few things I remember about that day. The details have faded over time, but the emotions remain vivid. The combination of joy, pain, and heartbreak created a moment that would shape me for many years to come.

I do not remember if my own mother came to visit. The few friends who did come had to be told that the baby—my baby—was not going to be coming home with me. I vaguely remember my dad and sister being there. When I was awakened in the middle of the next night with tremendous aching in my breasts and a soaked hospital gown, I did not even realize what was happening. No one told me that my milk would come in whether there was a baby to suckle or not. Thankfully, after ringing the call button, a kind and gentle nurse explained what was happening and brought me pills to help dry up the supply.

The physical pain was tough to manage, but the emotional pain was devastating. Shame, grief, and the feeling of being lost overwhelmed me. Not realizing it then, the numbing of my emotions began, like a frost settling in for the winter, going deeper and deeper, into my hurting heart. While my body endured the shock, my spirit struggled under the weight of loss and heartbreak.

Yet, amid the turmoil, one memory stands out—a small gesture of love that brought a touch of comfort. My grandmother had given me a beautiful blue housecoat specifically for my hospital stay, paired with a matching blue train case lined with a satiny interior. That thoughtful gift was one more act of kindness I can recall from that difficult night. A gentle reminder that compassion could still reach me even in the darkest moments.

The hardest part was the next few days. There are a lot of blank spaces in my memory of that time in my life. I do remember going to look through the nursery glass at my New Year's baby and seeing a tiny head covered in beautiful black hair. That was the last time I saw her for nearly 47 years. I wanted to die.

In fact, I faced death multiple times, both before and after that pivotal day—sometimes by my own hand and sometimes due to the actions of others. The first time I attempted suicide was at the age of eleven. My parents had divorced, and my mother had remarried, leading to a major upheaval in my life. Because my sister and I were the youngest of four, we were uprooted and moved to another province far away from everything familiar.

I still remember the day my mom arrived unexpectedly at school. She took me out of class without warning, announcing that she was taking my sister and me away—away from my beloved father, whom I adored, away from my two older siblings, and away from all the friends I had known my whole life. The suddenness and magnitude of the change were overwhelming, and that was when my emotions first began to numb.

My sister began to develop a close relationship with our stepbrother. While she found companionship in this newfound connection, my mother's attention was focused on her new husband, leaving me feeling increasingly overlooked. As those bonds formed around me, I was left on the periphery, struggling to find my place within our changed family dynamic.

This shift in relationships marked the beginning of a profound heartache. I remember the pain as something more than just emotional—it was a physical ache in my chest, a deep loneliness that settled inside me. For the first time in my life, I truly felt like an outsider, disconnected from the family I had once known. The sense of isolation and exclusion was overwhelming, leaving me to navigate these feelings on my own.

My stepdad and I did NOT see eye to eye, and I hated him. But for a good reason, it would seem. As it turned out, he was a pedophile who had abused his own daughter and who knows how many others. Years later, he was convicted and sentenced to a mere 2 years in prison where he was released much earlier due to good behavior! But that is a story for another time. But back to this time. I was so unhappy I decided I no longer wanted to live, so I took some pills I found in the medicine cabinet, wrote a goodbye note, and lay down on my bed to die. Fortunately, I got scared and managed to throw up. The Universe had other plans for me.

I excelled in sports and found confidence and friendship in that. My marks in school were exceptional, and my teachers loved me. I was finally starting to be happy again. But that all changed yet again when my mom and stepdad announced that we were moving back to my hometown. It was bittersweet, to say the least.

The next chapters of my life are when the memories get blurred and the timelines muddied. I know I went to live with my dad again and got tossed back and forth between my parents as they fought over who should have me, not who wanted me. I moved back and forth between my hometown and another town where my mom moved two hours away. Lots of drugs and alcohol came into play. When with my mom, I stole whatever pills I could find and took them just to see what might happen. Incredibly, the only reaction I ever remember having was a horrendous headache, accompanied by a deafening, buzzing noise in my head, that lasted for days. I remember taking a plastic tumbler, filling it up with straight alcohol—a little from each of my dad's bottles so he would not notice—and drinking them at lunch hour in Grade seven.

I am ashamed to say I was no longer the quiet, shy, obedient little girl I used to be. I became obnoxious, disruptive, and disrespectful in class. My teachers no longer loved me.

The last parent's home I lived in was back with my mom and stepdad. They were extremely strict and did not allow me much freedom. At least that is how I saw it. Living on a farm many miles from town was hard on a teenage girl. Friends were fickle, and you needed to stay in touch. Having snuck out of the house one night to meet friends on the backroads to go partying, my stepdad lay in wait for me. When I got home in the early morning hours, he ordered me to pack my bags and get out. I do not remember much of my mom in this situation. Grabbing whatever I could and stuffing it into a small black suitcase, I endured a very silent drive to town with my glaring stepdad. He dropped me off at the post office steps at 6:30 in the morning and told me good luck and goodbye. I asked him where I was supposed to go and what I was supposed to do. He just told me he didn't care.

Again, feeling lost and alone, I wandered down the dark street wondering what to do next.

I found myself at my older—and only— brother's doorstep. He was only twenty-one and was also working hard to make his way in the world. His home was a dilapidated cinderblock structure, known among locals as the "cardboard mansion." The front entry was nothing more than a wooden plank, and the back door was missing a doorknob. The chilly winter air blew freely through the basement's cracked blocks, creating little snowdrifts across my blankets. But in the summer, it was like air-conditioning so that was a plus. The basement floors were constantly damp and had become fertile ground for exceptionally large mushrooms that grew unchecked. Despite its rundown appearance this place became my refuge in a time of need. I am forever grateful to my brother for taking me in off the street.

When I had asked if I could stay there, my brother's only conditions were that I must graduate from high school, help with chores around the house, and get a job. I waitressed, cleaned rooms at a local hotel and worked on a cleanup crew for a house builder. I got particularly good at forging my mother's signature when I skipped school but still managed to graduate and received the Top Female Athlete of the Year award along with Most Improved Student.

However, a lot of drugs, alcohol, and partying went down in that old house. The atmosphere was often chaotic, with visitors drifting in and out. Amidst the constant activity, there were periods when food was scarce. I recall one particular time when the only things left to eat in the house were a stale bottle of salad dressing and a container of sauerkraut. That memory stands out as a stark reminder of how difficult and unpredictable daily life could be in that place. But it also makes me incredibly grateful for all the blessings I have now.

The first Christmas I spent alone was a deeply isolating experience, leaving me with an overwhelming sense of being lost and unwanted. The absence of family and the weight of loneliness pressed heavily on my heart during that season. In an effort to find solace amid the emptiness, I turned to music—drawn in by my brother's extensive record collection that filled the house with possibility.

With hours to fill and emotions to soothe, I found myself exploring a vast array of new music genres and artists. As I listened and learned, music became both entertainment and a source of comfort, helping me pass the time and offering a unique kind of companionship when I needed it most. I discovered a deep love for music, which provided a much-needed escape and a way to console myself as I navigated the challenges of being alone.

But booze and drugs were also my painkillers and sadly a lot of men took advantage of that and my young body, whether I was willing or not. I never told anyone. Shortly afterward, the inevitable happened and I found myself pregnant. I was terrified. But several weeks later, all alone in the house, I suffered a horrible miscarriage. All I remember was the excruciating pain and the excessive amount of blood. With no one to help me, I lay quietly on the dirty couch, feeling weak and tired and begged God not to let me die. I never went to a doctor or told anyone, and thankfully my angels were still there protecting me. I might not have realized I was being watched over at the time, but I certainly came to realize it many times later when my life once again was close to being taken.

I was looking for love in all the wrong places, as the song says, and the only way I knew to get love and affection was to give my body. I got pregnant again, and this time I was not 'lucky' enough to have a miscarriage. This baby was meant to be born!

I had one friend whom I had known since kindergarten. We were especially close, and her house was like a second home to me. Many of my early years were spent with that family, finding comfort and belonging within their walls. My heart was shattered when her mother learned about my situation and instead of offering understanding, she responded with rejection, banning me from their home and their lives. The pain was immense; her mother had once believed I could do no wrong, and now I felt as if I had been thrown away for a second time—discarded and unwanted, like a piece of garbage.

The heartbreak from that rejection haunted me for years. I was tormented by nightmares of abandonment and exclusion, not only by this woman but by others as well. I would wake up sobbing, overwhelmed by the pain that seemed impossible to escape. Sadly, these feelings followed me into adulthood. A heavy burden I carried long after the initial wound was inflicted.

I have come to understand the profound impact that words and actions can have on a person's life. Even a single moment of harshness or cruelty can leave scars that linger for years, shaping the way we see ourselves and the world around us. I have felt those marks— sometimes from the thoughtless words of others, sometimes from their actions—and I know how deeply they can hurt.

Yet, I have also discovered a beautiful contrast: encouragement and kindness possess a power just as strong as pain. The gentle words and compassionate gestures I received along the way have lifted me up, offering comfort and hope even in my darkest hours. These memories of kindness are a steady source of strength, reminding me that compassion truly has the ability to heal what rejection and cruelty once broke.

The following years are a blur of self-hatred and self-destruction. Drinking, partying, and regretting were the order of the day. I had given my baby away and did not know where or how she was. The last thing I learned was that she was having trouble breathing and had been flown to a major city 5 hours away. Now sixteen, I had moved out of my brother's house and in with my 23-year-old boyfriend who was extremely violent and abused me both emotionally and physically. My self-worth was at an all-time low. Yet I continued to press on.

During the two years I endured that relationship, death visited me repeatedly. My boyfriend was deeply troubled, often threatening not only his own life but mine as well. On several occasions, I found myself pleading with God for help, and time after time, my prayers were answered.

One particularly terrifying incident occurred when he was viciously strangling me. As I began to lose consciousness and believed my life was ending, something inexplicable happened—his arms suddenly flew backward, as if an unseen force had intervened and pulled him away. In that moment, I was certain that my angels were watching over me.

There was another frightening moment that remains etched in my memory. We were driving down the highway when my boyfriend, consumed by rage, began screaming that he was going to kill both of us. The tension in the vehicle was suffocating, and I feared for my life. Suddenly, out of nowhere, a coyote appeared on the road. My boyfriend struck the animal with the truck, which seemed to snap him out of his fury. He abruptly stopped the vehicle, got out, picked up the coyote from the highway, and threw it into the back of his truck, boasting about how much money he would make from selling its pelt. Strangely, that coyote became my saving grace that day. It felt as though my angels were still watching over me, intervening in the most unexpected way.

I made several attempts to leave him, desperately wanting to escape the cycle of abuse and fear. Each time, however, I was confronted by the harsh reality that I had nowhere permanent to go. The lack of a stable and safe place left me feeling hopeless and trapped, unable to break free from the hold he had over my life.

Finally, an exciting day arrived when my dad came to visit me and offered to pay my way to go to college in a nearby city. At last, it was a chance to escape. I applied for bursaries and scholarships with the help of another angel in my life, a high school teacher who saw the bruises and broken blood vessels in my eyes and took a special interest in me. She went out of her way to advise me in any way she could. I wonder if she may have called my dad to encourage him to help me. But I will never know the answer to that as they both have passed away.

I would like to say it was an easy transition to move away from my abusive boyfriend, but it was not. He was not willing to let go easily, threatening to commit suicide if I left. I never prayed so hard in my life for something **not** to happen, and thankfully it did not.

College years did not change me from the party girl that I was, but I got a part-time job and worked extremely hard to succeed. I was still starving for love and had little to no self-esteem. I dated a lot of guys and experienced a lot of heartaches. There was still so much shame and self-hatred covering me, and not realizing it, I wore it like a neon sign: Come abuse me, because I am worthless.

The years that followed were much happier. The Business Administration course I took at college had a work experience program that placed me at a local radio station. I tried my hand at writing commercials, then was hired in the traffic department operating a computer with a CPU the size of 3 or 4 refrigerators! How times have changed. I worked as an assistant but soon became the traffic manager. Still searching and feeling restless, I handed in my notice as I wanted to go back to college. I was offered the position of Promotions Director, so I stayed. This station had never had one before, so I was given the opportunity to create the job from the ground up. I had such little self-esteem and was painfully shy. That job forced me out of my shell and the real me started to emerge. Or at least a masked, happy version of me. It was truly fun! To get paid to promote was amazing. I remember one of my co-workers asking me if I ever stopped smiling. I was finally happy, but not yet healed.

I continued to party hard and there were many times I did not even remember driving home from a drunken night out. Thank God I never killed anyone else or myself. Once I even showed up to work totally out of it as I had gotten in at 5:30 a.m. and did not want to miss work, so I went in anyway. My angels were still with me, and some fellow co-workers snuck me out the back and covered me for that day. I am embarrassed to say that there were other similar instances.

The voice of suicide came back with a vengeance. I fought it so hard. I remember pacing and wrestling with that voice in my apartment one night, wanting to end it all, but I did not want to hurt my dad. That is what kept me going and kept me from leaving this world.

Unfortunately, that ugly, taunting voice kept screaming at me for many more years and still does, thankfully not as loudly.

I stayed in radio for 5 years then abruptly decided to leave and become a certified fitness instructor. At the time I had been living with and engaged to a guy I thought I loved, but also felt I was not good enough for. He was not physically abusive, but he was very controlling and particularly good looking. Why would someone like that want someone like me? I found myself extremely jealous, because I was so insecure. That caused us both a lot of frustration and pain. The restlessness returned, and I ended the engagement. I moved out into a basement suite of someone who happened to be a city employee... another angel placed in my life who helped me get some more education in that field and encouraged me to take a correspondence course on Fitness and Nutrition and became certified in that as well. That person even helped me write up a resume to apply for city jobs. I got the position of manager at a fitness facility. I also taught five and six classes per day and started to get quite burnt out.

The drinking and drugs continued as did the heartaches and regrets. The self-hatred was still alive and extraordinarily strong. I became obsessed with my weight. If I ate a cookie, I would have to go for a run no matter what. I even tried throwing up after each meal, but again I was being watched over because I hated throwing up and could not continue with that particular form of self-torture. Teaching fitness really saved my life as it was a great outlet for me. But due to my wounding, I got fed up one day and quit. That same day I got a call to sell advertising for a local newspaper which I happily accepted. The Universe still had my back.

In 1985 I met and married a guy I felt was "safe". He adored me, but we were like oil and water and did not mix. We brought out the worst in each other, and I was not emotionally able to really love anyone else let alone myself. We drank and partied and fought a lot! We were just on the verge of breaking up when my mom and stepdad came back into my life. They told us they had become "born-again" and that we needed Jesus too, and we must get married as we were 'living in sin.'

I saw the changes in them but then again, I had not seen them in years, and my stepdad was an expert manipulator and an exceptionally smooth talker. I had longed for a mother-daughter relationship, so we went along. We invited Jesus into our lives and hearts, started attending a local church and even got baptized. I really did have a sense of relief and peace, but my inner wounding and pain did not magically go away either.

We started spending a lot of time with my mom and stepdad. There was a lot of talk about demons and the devil, and I lived in absolute terror. All sorts of strange things happened during that time, and it took me several years to get fully free of my terror of being alone. Each unsettling experience reinforced my fear, making it difficult for me to trust that I could ever feel truly safe or secure on my own.

Over time, however, I slowly began to break free from the grip of this terror. It was a gradual process, marked by small steps toward gaining my independence and confidence. Eventually, I was able to overcome my fear of solitude but not for many more years.

I seemed okay on the surface, but I really was not. I tried so hard to fit in with the church people and create the perfect white picket fence family, but you cannot fit a square peg in a round hole. I did not fit in, hated the hypocrisy I saw and did not 'get' a lot of what was being taught. It just never sat right with me. We bounced from church to church looking for answers. Although along with the hypocrisy I also saw genuine love and caring for others in all the churches we attended. The hole in my heart was just too big and needed to be filled in other ways.

Pregnant with our first child, we ended up joining a religious cult, quit our jobs, sold our vehicles, got rid of all personal belongings and ties to the 'world' which included friends and family, except of course my mom and stepdad. He just happened to be the leader of the cult. But that is a story for another time.

Having escaped from the cult and come back to the real world, it took us some time to get our footing again. There were many people from the churches we had attended that came forward to offer love and support along with my two wonderful sisters, and without them life would have been much more difficult. I had believed I was condemned to never have a child again, because I had given my first daughter away, but in the years following, we were blessed with three beautiful daughters. Even though I was once again estranged from my mother, our precious girls were spared the abuse of a convicted pedophile. I considered that to be a bittersweet miracle.

In 1994, while pregnant with our third daughter we decided my husband needed to go to Bible School to become a pastor. Again, with blind trust we sold our home in the city and moved to a small town where the Bible school was located. Many miracles took place during that time. I remember praying for the money to pay the mortgage one morning and someone appeared at the door with the exact amount. People brought food, clothing, toys for my children and so much more, just when we needed it. Despite the blessings and support, I felt terribly alone, insecure, and lost. I was afraid to let anyone get too close to me for fear of being hurt. Suicidal thoughts were still present, and I had sunk into a deep postpartum depression. There were days when I could barely get off the couch, but I still wore the mask of a competent capable wife and mother.

I was asked to speak at ladies' gatherings and in churches to share my testimony. On the morning of one of those talks, I spoke about the pain of giving up my daughter for adoption. After returning to my seat, a woman sitting behind me gave me a heartfelt hug and confided that she had gone through the same experience. She shared how she had found her child and described the process she followed. Her story planted a seed of hope in me, and in the days that followed, I began to contemplate what finding my own daughter might look like. With three daughters of my own, I wondered how such a reunion would unfold and what impact it might have on our lives.

Less than a week after that pivotal moment, another miracle unfolded. An ad appeared in the local newspaper of the town where I once lived, seeking the birth mother of Dana Marie, born on January 1, 1978. By a stroke of luck, my sister—who still resided in that town— spotted the notice and passed the information on to me.

My heart raced and my hands shook as I prepared to write a response. With no name to address, I carefully composed a letter to the provided address, directed to the care of "Dani's mom" at a lawyer's office. Her adopted parents had renamed her Danielle, Dani for short. The waiting period for a reply felt interminable, filled with anticipation and anxiety.

When the reply finally arrived, it brought an overwhelming sense of relief and joy. Tears of happiness streamed down my face as I learned that my daughter was alive, healthy, and had been welcomed into a loving family. However, the next letter I received carried a vastly different tone. In it, her anonymous mother conveyed that my daughter was not interested in meeting me. Although I would later discover, more than thirty years afterward, that this was not the truth. At the time the message was devastating.

With that painful revelation, I was forced to bury my longing for reunion even deeper, clinging to the hope that someday she would want to meet me. The knowledge that my daughter was alive was a consolation, but it also unleashed a torrent of distress and agony that had been bottled up for years. My heart grew heavier, and I found myself sinking further into depression, weighed down by the emotional aftermath of this experience.

I had stopped drinking several years prior and tried to become the perfect wife and mother, but too many unhealed wounds were still oozing. I went for years of various forms of counseling, read self-help books, took numerous courses but the voices inside my head still tortured me.

Eighteen years went by along with some very tumultuous times. We moved a total of ten times during those years, also hopping from church to church, adding even more upheaval to an already unstable environment for my daughters. The generational wounds followed us, and all three girls were estranged from me at one time or another. Their teenage years were some of the toughest of my life and I am sure theirs as well. I used to take the full brunt of responsibility for this, but I now realize that there were many other contributing factors. The pain and heartache of having failed at both marriage and parenting was the breaking point of our family. I was no longer attending any church as I realized structured religion is a whole lot different from the spirituality I was seeking. We agreed divorce was the only answer even though it was crushing to realize how much our children would be hurt by this decision.

One of the greatest regrets of my life is the pain I have caused my own daughters. The wounds I inflicted upon them are still in the process of healing. I am deeply aware of the challenges they have faced as a result of my struggles.

My middle daughter, who has just recently been diagnosed with autism, was the first to start the healing process in our family. She bravely called out both of us, her parents, on how she had felt growing up and some of the wounds we had caused her. I realized she didn't want me to make excuses for my behaviours. She just wanted to be heard and for that wisdom I am profoundly grateful. I was able to have an open and honest discussion with her and to apologize for my role in her pain. She too has gone through years of counselling and inner healing.

As I continue to heal, grow, and evolve, I have watched ALL my daughters journey alongside me, finding their own paths to healing as well. I share openly that I am continuing on my healing journey and try to lead by example. By the grace of God

(Goddess), we have great relationships today, and for that I am profoundly grateful. Yet, I recognize that the healing process is ongoing for all of us, and I remain committed to supporting them as we move forward together.

There is so much more I could tell you here but again, those are chapters for another book.

Now, more than thirty years later, I am happily remarried to an incredibly generous, kind, and loving man. At this point we have seven children and eleven grandchildren between the two of us. The early years of our marriage were far from easy, as I was still grappling with deep emotional wounds from my past and dealing with the challenges of a blended family. Despite all this, my husband showed remarkable patience and strength, supporting me through my struggles and standing by my side when I needed it most.

Our story together is rich and complex, with many chapters that remain untold for now. Throughout this journey, I have continued to grow and heal and trust that something much bigger than me is overseeing it all.

Throughout all this time, I never gave up hope of finding my lost daughter. It was in 2016 when I submitted my DNA to a company that connects people with genetic relatives, holding onto the possibility that it might help me locate her. The hope of reunion remained alive in my heart, and I never stopped wondering about her well-being or where she might be.

It was December 10, 2023, seven years since I had submitted my DNA in the hope of finding my daughter. That evening, my husband's brother was visiting from southern Alberta. As they became engrossed in conversation, I took the opportunity to quickly check my emails. I was accustomed to receiving messages notifying me of new DNA relatives, though none had ever been the one I was longing for.

When I saw an email with the familiar subject line, I assumed it would be no different than the others. However, upon opening it, I read the words: "You have a 50% DNA match with this person who is your daughter." I sat there, stunned, and unable to fully process what was happening. To say I was shocked would be an understatement.

With hands trembling and my pulse racing, I excused myself from the conversation, claiming I was tired and heading to bed. Alone in my bedroom, sitting on the edge of my bed—literally on the edge of my seat—I found myself struggling with a whirlwind of emotions. Shock, disbelief, happiness, excitement, nervousness, and the pain from the past all surged to the surface, tangling together like a big knot in my stomach. I wanted to pour out my heart to her; tell her I was sorry and ask her to please forgive me and not judge me or hate me. I was hoping she would be happy she found me and that finding me might relieve her of any feelings of rejection or hurt she may have held. My biggest fear was that she would hate me and not want anything to do with me.

The commonsense part of me told me to just sleep on it and send a response in the morning, but the mother's heart in me knew I wouldn't get a wink of sleep if I didn't at least put something in writing. I kept it short and sweet, not wanting to put any pressure on her whatsoever:

"Hello Danielle. Words cannot express how it felt to see your name along with "daughter" come up in my list of DNA relatives. I have never stopped thinking and wondering about you for the past 45+ years. I was only fifteen when I got pregnant with you and I am truly hoping we can communicate in any way that would be comfortable for you. I hope to hear from you so we can talk more."

It was a long and agonizing three weeks before I finally received a response from my daughter., I could hardly think of anything else, feeling suspended between hope and uncertainty. As it turned out, she had not been actively searching for me. The DNA test kit that led to our connection was a thoughtful gift from a friend, intended to help her gain insight into her health issues. Neither of us could have anticipated that this gesture would result in us finding each other after so many years apart.

It wasn't until several months later that we were finally able to meet face to face. Both of us share a love for the outdoors, so my daughter suggested we get together on some walking trails near her home. The idea was to walk and talk, giving us space to connect in a natural and comfortable setting.

The encounter was nothing like the reunion I had pictured in my mind. I was mindful not to let my emotions overwhelm her, knowing how intense this moment was for both of us. We had already exchanged photographs, so I recognized her resemblance to myself—and even more strikingly, to my older daughter. Looking at her, it was as if they could have been twins.

Our embrace was calm and quiet, at least outwardly. Despite our composed appearances, we were both trembling, like shivering puppies. Trying to hold it together and remain strong, I felt like I was living in a dream, not fully able to grasp or comprehend the depth and breadth of what was happening. For so many years this was an untold story of my life, one I had carefully hidden and never talked about with anyone other than my closest family. I am grateful that I had already spoken to my daughters and my husband about her in advance. Because of this, the news was not an utter surprise when I finally told them. Their understanding and support made the process less daunting and helped ease the transition into this new reality.

The intensity of emotions I felt was unlike anything I had ever experienced. The closest analogy is that of a pressure cooker or a radiator filled with steam, where feelings have been simmering beneath the surface for years, contained by a strong, protective lid. If all that emotion were to be released at once, the force could be overwhelming—potentially even harmful to myself and those around me.

It became clear that, in order to process these powerful emotions safely, I needed to loosen the cap gradually. Our bodies are remarkably resilient, and I believe this slow release was a necessary way to protect myself and others from the full impact. Although I did not consciously set out to control these feelings, I instinctively knew I could not manage all of them at once. Instead, I had to let them emerge slowly, giving myself time and space to adjust and heal.

The shock and disbelief we both felt upon reconnecting were overwhelming. It was as if I were living in a dream—an experience so surreal it was hard to grasp. With this reunion, a flood of emotional pain rose to the surface, manifesting itself in physical symptoms. I had read about such reactions in the book *The Body Keeps The Score,* by Bessel Van Der Kolk, M.D., and had encountered similar reactions when I learned of my own mother's passing. The intensity of these emotions reminded me that the body often holds onto past trauma, resurfacing in moments of profound significance.

Despite the emotional pain and turmoil that surfaced during our reunion, the sense of relief and joy I experienced was profound. These feelings far outweighed any distress that tried to re-emerge from the past. The moment was made even more meaningful when my daughter revealed that she herself was a mother to a fourteen-year-old daughter—my granddaughter. This news was both overwhelming and deeply heartwarming, adding a layer of surprise and happiness. The revelation brought with it a sense of unexpected blessings, expanding my family in ways I never could have imagined and filling my heart with gratitude.

At present, we are slowly getting to know each other, navigating this new and unfamiliar terrain with trust in the Universe to guide us. The process of building our relationship is gentle and ongoing, as both of us adjust to this extraordinary development. My heart feels whole again, and for that, I am forever grateful.

Personal Reflection

Looking back on my journey, I am struck by the depth of pain and the heights of resilience that have shaped who I am today. The losses I endured—especially giving up my first child and surviving abuse—left wounds that took years to even begin to heal. For a long time, I felt defined by my trauma, loneliness, and the mistakes I made while searching for love and acceptance.

But through every dark chapter, I discovered small lights: the kindness of a nurse, the encouragement of a teacher, the support of family, friends and strangers who showed up when I needed them most. These moments reminded me that even in the bleakest times, hope can be found.

I make a conscious effort to offer encouraging words to others whenever I can. I know firsthand how much a single act of kindness can mean, and I strive to be a source of support and positivity in the lives of those around me. Cherishing the moments when others showed me compassion, I hope to pass that healing forward, knowing that even small gestures can make a lasting difference.

Healing has not been a straight path. There are still setbacks, relapses into old habits, and days when the clouds of depression loom above me. Yet, I am still learning to reach out for help, to accept support, and to forgive myself for not being perfect. Education, spirituality, and self-reflection are my tools for growth, helping me understand that my worth is not defined by my past.

I am grateful for the opportunities to rebuild my life, to find love again, and to see my children and grandchildren with greater compassion and awareness. I've learned that it's okay to ask for help, to set boundaries, and to let go of shame. My story is proof that survival is possible, and that joy can return even after years of sorrow.

"Out of difficulties grow miracles."
Jean de La Bruyere

My Affirmation

I am precious and valuable.

Your Elevation

To anyone facing similar struggles: your pain is real, and your journey matters. Healing takes time, and it's normal to feel lost along the way. But you are not alone. Don't be afraid to reach out for help. There is strength in vulnerability, and there is hope in every new day. Hold onto your light, even when it feels dim. Miracles can grow from the hardest places.

CATHY MORRISON

Cathy Morrison is a passionate special education teacher/ counselor who specializes in helping children and families find their unique gifts to live their best life. When she's not helping children, you can find her working with animals at the local zoo. She lives in Nashville, Tennessee with her family who she loves fiercely. Graduating from Vanderbilt University, she holds a master's degree in education in Special Education/Guidance and Counseling. Debuting as an author, she hopes "Twelve Steps Home" will be an inspiration to others who have lost loved ones.

If you feel led, please reach out to her at: twelvestepshome@yahoo.com.

Twelve Steps Home

My journey to find hope and become a light for others.

by Cathy Morrison

"Hey Cathy, how many steps?"

The echo of the words drifted through my thoughts as I sat on the noisy radiator, hoping it would warm the chilly hospice room. Soft words came from the bed, where my dad held my mom's hand and gazed at her with the same love he always had. He loved to share the story of how he fell in love with her the day he gave her a juicy, red apple in the gym. A year after graduation, she agreed to marry him. The room felt familiar and comforting as I listened to them sharing memories about the love they built.

"Twelve," I said without thinking, then quietly hopped off the radiator. The moment grew heavy; my parents were sharing their last moments together. The chill made everything seem fragile. I tried not to imagine what tomorrow would bring.

"It's a bit farther than I thought. I guess I'll need my shoes then," Dad whispered with a smile.

I approached the bed, trying to ignore the despair in Mom's tired eyes. I managed to give her a brief smile and took her hand, calloused from years of gardening and taking care of the family. Her face, lined from laughter, looked pale as she recovered from another coughing spell. My heart ached as she squeezed my hand and adjusted her hot pink cap, covering her hair still regrowing from radiation.

Dad shifted his gaze from the ceiling to me, then nodded and closed his baby blue eyes. I wasn't sure what caught his attention, but I sensed we weren't alone, especially since I thought I heard a quiet male voice ask, "Is he here yet?" Ignoring the urge to look around, I tucked the colorful M&M blanket around Dad's cold feet.

"There you go; you're ready now," I whispered as I leaned down to kiss Dad on top of his snowy white hair.

"Time for you to take your mother home," he said softly. "She needs her rest."

Dad, known for his wisdom and measured words, was right. We all needed rest. The week had worn us down with long hospital days, endless tests, and constant doctor consultations. Moving Dad to a nearby hospice facility was tough. A conflict also arose between my parents. Dad wanted Mom to rest and recover from her cancer, but Mom insisted on staying by his side. They teetered on the balance of who should be there for the other through sickness and health. It was the very essence of their marriage vows, taken 66 years ago. Their arguments grew as Dad's heart condition worsened.

My mind raced, desperate for last week's normalcy, as I wished time would stand still. Just four days earlier, everything changed with an early morning phone call. As memories of that morning surfaced, I recalled seeing it was Mom calling and I answered as usual.

"I love you more," I said, trying to appear awake and chipper.

"I love you, too, but your dad wants to go to the emergency room. His legs don't want to work anymore," Mom quickly replied.

"Call 911. I'll be right there," I said, trying to calm the emotional whirlwind inside me.

I jumped out of bed and pulled on my dirty jeans. I rushed next door as fast as I could. My heart pounded with fear and worry. As I left the comfort of my home, a deep sense of dread began to grow. Dad had promised never to go back after his long hospital stay last year.

Running through the backyard, I felt anxiety shouting inside me, "This is it! My biggest fear, losing them, is coming true."

Not knowing what to expect, I opened the back door with trepidation. I saw the paramedics coming in the open front door. Without taking time for social greetings, I guided them through my childhood home to my parents' sanctuary, their private bedroom.

We entered the bedroom to see Mom frowning and shouting at Dad, "YES, I am going with you! No one should die alone!"

"Whoa! Who said anything about dying? I think we're getting ahead of ourselves," the medic intervened, trying his best to diffuse the tension in the room. "Let's take a look and see what's going on."

"Maybe you should be checking her out instead of me," Dad quipped. "She's been up all night coughing from pneumonia. She has no business going with me. She needs her rest."

I wrapped a blanket around Mom's shoulders and helped her to a chair.

"Why don't you sit here and make sure they're taking care of him?" I told Mom as I gathered Dad's things.

From the many hospital treks, I knew he would need his insurance card and driver's license. As I pulled his ID from his wallet, an old, tattered picture fell out and landed facedown. I reached for the photo and saw the word "HOME" written in Dad's meticulous handwriting.

"HOME" was such a simple word yet held so much emotion. The image pulled me back to my first home in Germany, shortly after my parents married and Dad enlisted in the army. In that flashback, I remembered their humor: while most people brought back Hummels or cuckoo clocks, they brought back me. Home is where I learned how humor helps us through life's difficulties.

Turning the photo over in my hands, my heart filled with love and warmth. I was looking at a snapshot of Dad and me on a California beach when I was three years old. I suddenly realized that not only did my dad love me, but I was also his HOME.

A rapid knock jolted me back to the hospice room, pulling me back to the present. Memory and reality blurred like mist rising from a lazy river on a foggy day. The intake nurse entered, asking if we were spending the night with Dad. Refocusing, I glanced at the white clock above the door: 8:12—eight hours since we checked in at noon. Again, I noticed how often the number "12", a master number of completeness, appeared during our journey.

Dad quickly opened his eyes and pointed over to me, "That one can."

Then he shook his finger toward Mom, eyes brimming with tears. "But this one needs to go home and get some rest to kick her lung cancer."

Mom looked over at me helplessly, silently begging me to intervene. Thankfully, the nurse invited us to follow her to gather bedding.

Leading us to a nearby couch, the nurse gently told Mom, "I know you really want to stay with him. Often, our loved ones wait for the ones they love the most to leave before they go. It is his way of protecting you."

A tear rolled down Mom's cheek as she nodded with a silent resolve.

She sighed, a resigned smile flickering across her face. "Well... he's always been stubborn like that! If that's what he wants..." Her voice faded.

Later that night, when I returned to Dad's room, the number 12 caught my eye on the door. He was lying so still that my heart skipped a beat. Not sure what I would find, I leaned in to kiss him on his forehead, just like he kissed me when I was little.

I let out a sigh of relief when I heard Dad clear his throat.

My heart sank when he said, "I hope heaven is as good as they say it is."

"Oh, Dad, it is so much better than you can even imagine," I replied. "I'm a little jealous that you get to go before me."

Dad's eyes popped open, and he chuckled, "Well, it's only fair since I am a bit older than you. How do you know so much about it?"

I shared with him my near-death experience during a recent surgery. There are no words to explain the beauty and serene peacefulness of the place I visited. I would have loved to stay. However, I was told it wasn't my time yet. I still had family who needed me here.

Dad smiled and replied," You NEVER told me THAT! If you have any other secrets, now's the time. I feel myself fading."

I reached for Dad's hand and said, "It's time to rest now. By the way, I know where to find you if I need you. Did I ever tell you about the time your mother visited me in the garden last summer?'

Dad squeezed my hand a little tighter and closed his eyes as I shared about an astral visit I had with his mother, who passed in 1976. As I picked green beans, she appeared before me, thanking me for taking care of her baby, my dad. It felt like my grandmother's way of reassuring us that family was waiting for him on the other side.

Mom and the nurse re-entered the room as I was finishing the story. I was trying to hold back tears as Mom sat on the side of the bed. Sadness flooded through me as our time together was fleeing. I stepped back so Mom could say her final goodbyes.

Dad whispered, "I thought I told you to go home."

He then smiled and patted Mom's hand and said, "I love you more. Now go home."

After we left Dad at the hospice, the drive home was silent—a stark change from the emotional intensity of the day. My heart hurt as I watched Mom sleep, looking so fragile. I felt angry at how unfair life could be. How can you share a life and not be there at the end?

Exhaustion hit me like a ton of bricks when we arrived home. The day's events and emotions had caught up with me. When Mom asked me to rest with her for a bit, I agreed. Lying next to her, I was overcome by the deep comfort of being loved just as I am. It was the same feeling of HOME I had when I saw the photo of Dad and me.

I must have dozed off. Suddenly, I woke up, startled, to a phone ringing in the distance. The peace of brief sleep evaporated quickly as I read "Hospice House" on the screen.

A sense of dread filled my bones. Trying hard to fight back the scream that was building in my vocal cords, I heard a whispered "Hello? "slip from my lips.

The kind voice on the other end of the line said, "I'm sorry to inform you. Your dad passed peacefully in his sleep at 12:12."

Little did I know the significance of answering "12" to Dad's question earlier. Twelve seemed to show up as a sign of support, from the room where Dad passed to the times on the clock. The song *Will the Circle Be Unbroken* played in my mind. I suddenly realized Dad was the missing piece to his family circle. He was the youngest of ten children. With his parents, they made twelve. With his passing, he was the last to join them and complete the circle. The voice I heard in the hospice room was his family calling him home.

The events of the next week were a blur as we prepared for Dad's celebration of life ceremony. Winter weather in Nashville can be unkind. On the day of Dad's funeral, we woke to an icy fog and rain with temperatures dropping below freezing. Mom's cough was getting worse, yet she insisted on greeting everyone who came to pay their respects with her call sign, a big bear hug, and a warm smile.

By the end of the next week, the calls and visits slowed as everyone returned to their own lives. Mom and I were trying to stay strong for each other without Dad. The house felt so weird without him because HOME was his favorite place to be. Now it was a strange and painful place. I sat in his recliner, touching his knick-knacks, realizing that he would never touch any of them again. My mind could not comprehend that he would never sit there again. His empty chair at the table was a daily reminder that he was no longer there. The house was too quiet without his presence.

I thought about the beach photo and saw how meaningful it was. Dad was our anchor, Mom was our lighthouse, and I was the water connecting us. My parents had always been my safe place, but now we were lost in a storm without our anchor.

Grief hit us hard and filled our home with sadness. Losing Dad was painful, and I also had to comfort Mom as she lost her lifelong partner. Knowing home would never be the same, we tried to make new memories by doing things Dad usually didn't enjoy, like eating cereal for dinner and watching Hallmark movies. It didn't take away the pain, but it made the house feel a little less empty.

Mom's health continued to decline as her cough deepened, and my lighthouse was dimming right before my eyes. When I mentioned I was worried about her, she just said she was tired and needed more rest.

The cycle of the past week started to repeat itself as the phone rang early Sunday morning, waking me from a restless sleep. I answered the phone when I saw it was Mom.

"Cathy, I need to go to the emergency room. These coughing fits are taking my breath away, and I'm having chest pains."

I could see from her wheezing and the gray color of her skin that her pneumonia was getting worse. The doctors checked her charts and vitals, then admitted her to the same hospital where Dad had been just ten days before. My heart pounded in my chest as I waited for the test results. The fear of losing mom, too, was too much to bear.

I stayed with Mom for long past visiting hours, watching the Super Bowl with her, so she wouldn't be alone. At halftime, Mom hugged me a little tighter and insisted that I go home and get some rest. I reluctantly agreed, kissing her on the forehead and whispering, "I love you more" as I walked out the door.

The hospital called around midnight, telling me to return as soon as possible due to a "medical incident" with Mom. The details of the night still haunt me in my sleep. When I arrived at the hospital, I went immediately to the ICU. The doctor denied my entry, stating that the room where Mom was looked like a war zone due to blood loss. The wait was suffocating as the air around me turned frigid and the acrid smell of fear overcame my senses.

I had to rein in my anger when I was finally allowed to see Mom. There was no warning or preparation for me seeing Mom on life support, even though her chart specifically stated DNR (Do Not Resuscitate). My heart shattered as I saw her hooked up to a ventilator, breathing for her, and tied to IV lines and machines, forcing life-sustaining medications into her. When I demanded an explanation, I was simply told a nurse had discovered Mom unconscious and codes were called. I was outraged that no one had answers for me and felt so helpless in letting Mom down by not honoring her wishes of no life support.

After several hours of waiting and still no answers, I was at my wits' end. Even though I was already at my maximum capacity due to just losing Dad, I was adamant that Mom would receive the same level of compassion and care. I found myself at a horrendous crossroads, teetering on the edge between begging for doctors to save her and begging for the machines to stop.

Realizing that life doesn't deal with bargains, I decided to love her the only way I knew how, and that was by letting her go. My repeated request to cease life support was ignored by the entire night shift. When the new shift of doctors arrived, I demanded to speak to an administrator, who finally agreed to my request.

A grueling and cruel 36 hours later, I had to stifle my heartbreak and do what was best for Mom. Overcome with helplessness and despair, I held my precious Mom's hand and told her it was okay for her to go with Dad as I tearfully disconnected the machines that were holding her here. It was time for her to go home.

The hardest walk I ever had to take was to walk out of the hospital without her. Two weeks ago, we had walked together behind Dad on his Veteran's Escort of Honor, but now I was alone. There is something very cruel in losing the very person who has always helped me survive this kind of pain.

People often ask how I manage to survive losing both of my parents in such a brief time. Honestly, I do not know except that something greater than me gave me the strength to keep going. Some people call it resilience; I call it survival.

I had no fuel left in my emotional tank. I was an abandoned orphan whose story died with them. I could not imagine life without the people who loved me first. They were my Home, my anchor, and my lighthouse. Now I had to figure out how to navigate in a world I never wanted, a life without them.

In the immediate aftermath of my parents' deaths, I kept myself busy so I could not feel the pain. Their home was filled with all the things we leave behind when we die. In addition to rehoming their belongings, there were numerous meetings and a substantial amount of paperwork to complete to ensure their final wishes were fulfilled. Exhaustion and defeat quickly settled in as I hit roadblock after roadblock. My innate resilience had run dry, and everything came to a screeching halt. I woke up one morning with the brutal realization that their deaths were not a bad dream; they were my reality. It was the day I learned what heartbreak really meant.

The burnout from not taking the time to stop and do what I

feared the most and really grieve their loss took its toll. I thought grief was something to be conquered, to be pushed through and packed neatly away; however, I found out grief was a strange visitor that I didn't recognize. It didn't show up as sadness and tears; in fact, it took me over a year to cry for my parents. It manifested as anger, exhaustion, disconnection, and even a smile when I was breaking inside. Each holiday and milestone of their birthday and death triggered such intense pain. I found myself angry when my daily phone calls to check on them or ask for advice went unanswered. I was plagued by insomnia, dreading sleep because of the incessant dreams of hearing the machines that kept Mom alive. My anxiety levels were off the charts. I became hypersensitive to sounds and smells due to the trauma of hospice and hospital settings.

The mask of being strong and having it all under control was crumbling. The mental and physical exhaustion made it so that I couldn't find a way to accept the help and support of my friends and family. It was like I was suspended in space inside a frozen iceberg, watching the lifeboats pass me by. I desperately wanted to move forward, yet I found myself clinging to the pain because it felt like it was all I had left of my parents.

I cried out, 'THIS ISN'T FAIR!' but there was only silence. I kept asking myself questions full of guilt and shame: 'Why?' 'What if?' and 'If only.' My efforts to hold it all inside began to lose their grip, giving way to numbness and apathy. I had never felt grief like this before. It was so heavy that every day was a struggle. I was completely lost and broken, frozen without the capacity to love. I lost the will to live and wanted it all to stop. The deeper I sank, the more intense my yearning to give up and die with them.

Even in my darkest moments, I remember seeing hope in my family's caring eyes. I knew I had to find the courage to keep living. It was like hearing a siren of hope calling me home over the mournful sound of homesickness my parents had left behind. That was my sign that it was time to do more than just survive. It was time to start living again.

Not knowing where to start, I relied on the roadmap my parents had instilled in me. In a rush to numb the pain, I forgot how important it was to connect with a higher power. Sure, I would say a quick blessing before meals, but I often missed the chance to really commune with God. I needed to remember that all relationships, whether earthly or heavenly, require nurturing to grow.

Over the years, my relationship with God has been complex. My parents were devout in their faith, and I tried to follow their example; however, like many, I had to find my own way. I've always tried to please everyone, to be strong and put others first, like an oak tree that never breaks.

My parents' deaths were the storm that nearly broke me. In searching for help, I did not find God on a church pew; I found her in the middle of my pain and grief, in the quiet moments when I was depleted and exhausted from giving myself away.

One night, I recall crying out as I washed my face, getting ready for bed. It was a cry of anguish and despair as I let out the unbearable load I had been trying to carry for so long.

"God, I'm handing my life to you because I AM DONE! ... You either take me from this life, or you have to make everything that I have lived through and gone through mean something, because I CANNOT do this anymore!"

I'm not sure how long I lay on the cool tile floor of the bathroom. I remember looking at the far corner of the ceiling. Since I didn't hear a faint voice asking, "Is she here yet?" I knew I had to find my own strength.

As I tried to calm my breathing, I whispered, "I don't want to break. Please show me the way home." Slowly, I began to feel a gentle sense of peace and a deep knowing inside me.

"I AM! I always have been! I always will be! Cathy, you've got peace like a river flowing through you; let it heal you."

I found myself thinking, "I guess God really does know my name after all!"

The visit humbled me. Who am I to tell God that I am not enough? In that moment, I surrendered and let go of the grief and control. It was a big step for me, since I was always the one who had it together and kept everything in control. I was the one who took care of everyone else. Before, I always told myself, "I got this!" but now I had to admit, "I don't have anything." I realized I was nothing without the creator who made me.

Rising from the bathroom floor, I subconsciously heard Mom's voice say, "You can't break a woman who draws her strength from God." I smiled as I remembered her reciting, "*God is within her; she shall not fail.*" (Psalms 46:5) to me when life would get tough.

Standing on the promise that we are not alone, I began to open up to the love and support that surrounded me. The silence and absence of losing my parents carved out a space inside me that only I could step into. It was time to start my own resilience journey, one step at a time, back home.

First, there was the awareness and acknowledgement of the need for help finding light in the darkness. By admitting that grief was overtaking my life, I was able to see how being broken allowed light to come in.

Next, there was Hope. I began to believe that there was something better than suffering and had to find the courage to face what seemed impossible. Even when I wanted the pain to end, I still felt a spark of hope. My desperate plea to God in the bathroom turned into a glimmer of hope that light would eventually come.

Once I started wanting peace, I sought help by talking to friends and reaching out to professionals. Caring counselors helped me get back on track toward love, acceptance, and purpose. Facing our fears is hard and realizing things aren't okay can feel overwhelming. Instead of hiding from my feelings, I let myself pause and feel the emotions of my parents' deaths within the safety of those whom I trusted.

When I started to trust that I was safe, I began the liberating process of letting go of needing to control everything. Until my darkest night on the tile floor, I felt I had to be strong for everyone around me. And I was, until I couldn't be anymore. I had to let myself break and allow my loved ones to see me raw and vulnerable so I could move forward in my healing.

Next, I had to be honest with myself, my thoughts, and my actions before I could start to heal. Grief made me examine my weaknesses and strengths, allowing me to start the challenging work of taking care of myself. It was time to stop neglecting myself and extend the same compassion I offer others to myself.

My first act of self-care was to forgive myself— for the things left unsaid to my parents, for the things I said and now regret, for not valuing my life, and for wanting to end the precious gift they gave me. I also had to forgive myself for neglecting my own needs for others and, most importantly, for not trusting the little girl in the photo.

To forgive myself at this level, I had to rely on God to help me see myself through His eyes and love myself as He loves me. My soul needed quiet time alone with God. I remembered reading that any meditation is helpful, so I promised myself to spend time in prayer every day. At first, I just sat in silence, but I kept at it. By talking to my Creator daily, I have learned that grief and gratitude can coexist. I could miss the love I lost and still be thankful for the love I had. Gratitude helped chase away the darkness of grief.

As I prayed more, I realized I missed feeling grateful for the little things. Committing to writing in a gratitude journal as a daily habit helped me reconnect with my higher power. At first, I stared at a blank page, struggling to feel grateful for anything. One day, I saw a bird on a wire and wrote, "I'm thankful for birds." Each day, my list grew as I looked for good things.

Slowly, the feeling of being at home and loved returned to my daily life. I started to prioritize and intentionally choose to do the things I used to take for granted. One of the hardest things was learning to say no when people expected me to say yes. I had to set boundaries and prioritize myself. I began drinking more water, eating better, and taking daily nature walks.

Then it was time to share my story so others could heal from my pain. I guess that's what happens when I tell God to take me or make life mean something.

Little by little, I started to feel stronger as life settled into a new routine. Sitting with my grief was hard, but it was necessary for healing. As I let myself feel, I found it easier to accept help from family and friends. I began to notice small signs of hope around me, like finding a coin in the parking lot or hearing a mourning dove outside my window. Laughter slowly returned to our family, especially when the new grandbaby arrived. I found myself sitting in Mom's seat at the table, as if she were passing her role as the family lighthouse to me. I am finally ready to be home for the people who love me.

My Affirmation

Walk on. Walk on, with hope in your heart. You'll never walk alone. (*Rogers and Hammerstein, Carousel 1945*)

Your Elevation

My "Why?" for taking the leap of faith and writing this story is so that you know that you are not alone. We all need others – family, friends, and/or spiritual support—to help us find our way. As I started this grief journey, I wish I had known support was always with me. It is there for you too. How quickly it is to isolate within a cocoon when we lose those we love. The cocoon may be necessary to process the loss; however, while we are immersed in the darkness, the light is waiting for us. Keep your sights on the beauty of the butterfly that will soon emerge. I hope this story helps you realize that support, earthly as well as heavenly, is always within your reach and is patiently waiting to help you to find your way to the light.

PATRICIA SCOTT

Patricia Scott is a muti-faceted Virgo Sun, Gemini Rising, who has explored life through a variety of jobs, vocations and experiences. A retired public school teacher, owner of a fitness business, a dance and yoga instructor, a singer, a performer, a college writing teacher, a Martha Beck certified life coach as well as a wife, mother and grandmother of two beautiful boys who call her CeCe. She holds a Master's Degree in Creative Non-fiction Writing from Northern Michigan University, having written her thesis about her last year of teaching middle school entitled The Eighth Grade Dance. She is a die-hard Detroiter and a permanent resident of her beloved state of Michigan. She can be reached at soulscriptcoaching@gmail.com

An Inconvenient Grief

Finding Solace in the Deep River of the Soul

by Patricia Scott

I was five years old. This is how I remember it:

I woke up from a sound sleep to my mother screaming: shrill and loud.

"The baby's dead; the baby's dead! No, no, no, he's not moving. Clyde, the baby's dead."

Light shone underneath my bedroom door, so I slipped out of bed. I wanted to see my mother, to see if the baby in her belly was really dead. I was scared. Opening the door, the bright light in the hallway surprised me, but there was my dad, standing in the doorway of my parent's bedroom, stark naked, his robe shrugging up over his shoulders.

"Go back to bed, right now. And stay there," he said harshly. And I ran back into my bed and pulled up the covers. My bedroom door closed firmly, shutting out the light.

I heard all kinds of things as I lay in the dark. My mother, now wailing and crying. A big crash, like someone falling down the stairs, voices, my brother in the hallway, my father on the phone. I didn't dare move.

Who killed the baby?

My mother had told me, that very day, that if the baby was a boy, his name would be Harold. A nursery had been assembled with a crib, a changing table and curtains at the windows. For weeks, I had gone into that room to feel the sheets and count the stacks of cloth diapers with their rubber pants; I longed for him. I was excited to be a big sister and I knew that I would be his best friend.

I had a Hedda get Bedda doll, a baby doll with three different faces that I could change by turning a knob on the top of her head. I pretended that she was my baby for real. When I talked to her, I imagined Harold, yet unborn, "I will love you. I will take care of you," I said as I cradled Hedda, turning her face so that she was sick, then well, then sleeping.

Did Daddy do something to the baby?

Downstairs the doorbell rang, startling me. It was Mrs. Bentel from across the street, and I could hear the three of them murmuring in the living room. Moments later, flashing red lights struck my bedroom walls and I sat up to see an ambulance in the street in front of the house. My heart was pounding. More talking, stranger's voices now, voices over a radio and static. I looked out the window, even knowing that I would be in trouble if my dad looked up and saw me. My mother lumbered to the back of the ambulance and the two ambulance guys helped her up, where she disappeared inside. As they were pulling away, my father backed down the driveway in our car. I could hear Mrs. Bentel in the kitchen putting on the kettle.

Sometime later, I fell asleep.

In the morning, my father was slumped at the kitchen table drinking a cup of Sanka. He told me and my brother to get ready for school, and that the baby had been a boy and that he had died. He would pick Mother up at the hospital later that day, and that we needed to be quiet when we got home. And with that, we both went upstairs to change into the school clothes that we had laid out the night before. I remember Mrs. Bentel silently brushing my hair into a pony tail. We ate some toast and bowls of Cheerios, and walked to school. When we got home, the house was silent. Our mother was in her bed asleep. We were quiet.

There was no funeral for Harold; my parents went by themselves to bury him one day when we were at school. We never spoke of him again. It would be another 40 years before I would find him in the cremation wall of the White Chapel Cemetery. They hadn't put his name on his plaque; it simply read 'Baby Boy Scott'.

Around the same time, but before Harold died, my parents had taken us on a rare family outing to see the movie, Peter Pan, starring Mary Martin. It was a big deal. They bought the album as well, and afterwards, I spent many hours in the living room, playing the record on the stereo, singing the songs and acting out scenes from the movie. After Harold died—a stillbirth—I developed a Peter Pan phobia, an anxiety that made it impossible to fall asleep. At night, I would lay in bed, terrified that Captain Hook's pirate ship would sail up to my bedroom window and that I would be taken away to Never Never Land, where I would never grow up, 'never grow up, not me'.

In her book, *The Language of Emotions*, sociologist and educator, Karla McLaren, says that grief is "The Deep River of the Soul," that acknowledges and integrates our profound losses into our lives. She illuminates how woefully inadequate our culture's grief rituals are: either engaging one's mental intellects about the why of the loss: 'illness', 'treatment', 'hospitals', or other's religious/metaphysical intellect: 'gone to a better place', 'there is no death'—to deny the loss entirely. In Western culture, we have hidden our messy, emotional experience of death with platitudes, busyness and stiff upper lips. And we grieve in silence.

At five, I didn't know what I was experiencing was grief, but I was sad. Mother found my sadness an affront: I didn't carry Harold in my belly; I never even saw him. Harold was with Jesus; how could I be anything but happy for him? And furthermore, how did I think she felt, giving birth to a dead child? I was filled with shame at my selfishness. Face red, my heart fluttering in my little chest, I looked down at the floor and cried silent tears.

There were no explanations, no hugs, no comfort. My parents' expectation for my brother and I was that we present as happy, smart and grateful. And so, I gathered myself up that day and presented as happy, smart and grateful. I made it a practice, an automatic response, no matter how I actually felt. It didn't work so well when I tried to fall asleep at night.

It wasn't until I was almost 60 that I first experienced grief as the deep river of the soul, with the death of my husband, Mark.

In college I tended bar and waited tables to pay my rent and expenses. On Sunday mornings, I was the opening manager of the Small Planet Vegetarian Restaurant, and I was in the restaurant by myself. I enjoyed it—the quiet, the empty tables, and the faint, but bitter smell of stale beer and cigarettes from the night before. I dropped a cassette tape in the player, adjusted the volume, and grabbing a tray, set out catsups and salt and peppers on the tables. I unlocked the front door after I started the coffee.

On this particular Sunday, it was snowing lightly, and a small gust pushed grey flakes down Albert Street. I heard the door open, felt the burst of cold, and in walked a tall man wrapped in a red scarf, jeans and hiking boots.

"You open?" he asked as he began to unwind the scarf from his face.

"He's gorgeous", I thought, and my heart was loud as I walked towards him, still holding the tray.

"The cook isn't here yet; you'll have to wait if you want something to eat. Shouldn't be long," I said. "There's fresh coffee."

"How 'bout that, I just want coffee. Two cups to go, if you do that."

"I do that; have a seat."

He sat at a table across from the bar. I found the cups and the lids stacked in a cupboard above the wait station, grabbed a couple white plastic creamers from the walk-in and headed back into the dining room, heat in my face.

It had been a rough year. Separated from a short and intense relationship that produced one small son, I was in the middle of a painful breakup, and in walks this beautiful man asking for coffee in a Sunday morning snow squall. I set the cups, now filled with steaming coffee, on the table in front of him. His eyes were kind, smile a little crooked. He made no move to stand.

"What's your name?" he asked.

We talked. He was from Boulder, Colorado, but had grown up here in East Lansing after his parents divorced and his mother drove cross country in a station wagon with five kids and a cat named Moe. She moved her family into his grandfather's house, the house in which she herself had grown up. In Boulder he cooked in a restaurant/ bar, and was a ski bum—his self-description— working just enough to support his obsession with two inches of fresh powder. He lived in a party house called Club Zircon, with four other guys. At some point, I sat down.

But it was only a few minutes before patrons began wandering in for brunch. The cook had arrived and I could hear him rattling around in the kitchen. It was time to go to work.

As he stood to go, a coffee in each hand, he explained that his brother worked at Campbell's Smoke Shoppe, in the next block, and that the coffee was much needed. I got the impression there was a Saturday-night-into-Sunday-morning involved. I didn't charge him for the coffee.

He showed up again at four o'clock, when I had told him I got off work.

Later we would both say it was love at first sight. At our wedding, his Campbell's Smoke Shoppe brother, Christopher, said during his best man toast, that Mark had come into the smoke shop that day, set his brother's coffee on the glass counter and announced, "I just met the woman I am going to marry."

The following summer, he loaded his faded red Datsun pick-up with everything he owned and drove home to East Lansing. We were married a year later in his mother's backyard, the October autumn leaves providing the canopy. Our marriage lasted 22 years, but the relationship has lasted a lifetime and beyond.

I was 28 and he was 30 when Mark and I married, and we immediately went about the business of becoming adults. He got a job with the State of Michigan Department of Natural Resources as a recreational trail designer, and I went back to Michigan State University and earned a teaching certificate. I brought my four-year-old son, Michael, into the marriage, and we bought a house in town so that he could walk to school. I got a teaching job in a near-by school district that wanted to create a drama/theater program for middle school and high school. I had both education and experience in theatrical performance, and was hired in with a high school choir director to create a performance program. I taught drama at the middle school and directed two performances a year. It was a rare and rewarding job, and I felt lucky to have it.

Mark became my set designer and builder. He was a phenomenal visual artist, and a proficient wood worker, who could envision and create large sets, designed to be seen from the back of the house. We spent hours together pouring over scripts, mapping out the entrances and exits of the actors, experimenting with the lights in the booth for effect. Knowing how the actors would move, and where the lighting was best, he created sets from start to finish—from buying the materials to supervising parent volunteers on Saturday mornings with nails, hammers and paint brushes.

During a dress rehearsal for one of our shows, we sat rows up in the dark auditorium watching it run. He reached down and took my hand, giving it a slight up and down pump. I looked at him and smiled. We had done well.

We were very much a team, and very much in love. We had a full life. Michael had activities, and later athletic events that we participated in and attended. We camped and traveled the woods and white sand beaches of Michigan, and we became active members of People's Church—the original church in East Lansing where his mother had been a member for decades. We had friends in the neighborhood with whom we got together on Friday nights for end-of-the-week cocktails, while Michael played Capture the Flag with their sons in the neighborhood until after dark.

I knew Mark was a drinker from the beginning, but I was a drinker too and drinking alcohol, often to excess, was a normal aspect of our life. Everyone drank, our friends drank, our coworkers drank—it was simply a part of living. But as time went on, Mark, more and more, was displaying characteristics that frightened and enraged me. He hid to drink, and he hid how much he drank. He went away on weekends to drink, taking hunting and fishing trips with the guys. Over time it became apparent that Mark needed to drink.

When I discovered a secret wall of empty beer cans in the

basement, I finally realized that he had a problem. That weekend, we carried almost 400 empties out to recycling in black plastic bags. He was humiliated. I was angry. It would be more than a decade before I realized that I too had a problem with alcohol, but at this time, we were focused on him.

We went to marriage counseling, and at the suggestion of my close friend, Anne—whose husband had lost a job due to his drinking. I went to Al-Anon. I arrived at St. Thomas Aquinas church on a warm Sunday evening for my first meeting. Standing on the sidewalk outside the door, I was paralyzed, unable to open it. Walking through that door would mean it was true: I was married to an alcoholic. The enormity of that admission provoked anxiety and I was pacing back and forth, fighting tears. Finally, a man walked up.

"First meeting?" he asked and I nodded, looking down at the sidewalk. "Can I help?"

I gestured towards the door. He opened it, and I stepped through.

"I guess that wasn't so hard after all," I said, now crying but trying to make a joke.

"Everything about this is hard, but you got yourself here and now you're in the door," he said kindly. "Most people don't even show up. You've got the courage it takes to do this work. The program works if you work it. It'll take some time, but miracles happen. I promise."

He pointed me to the room where a circle of chairs had been set up and he turned and entered the AA meeting room across the hall. Looking over his shoulder, he motioned for me to take a seat. I was the 'newcomer.'

Al-Anon was an education for me and provided me with a community of supportive people who understood my pain due to their own struggles. In Al-Anon, I learned about alcoholism as a predictable set of thoughts and behaviors, and about my own co-dependance that was designed to manage the unmanageable. Most importantly, I learned that I was married to a good man who suffered from a disease, not a shithead who was out to hurt me.

Marriage counseling, on the other hand, was a disaster. Mark couldn't talk about what he was thinking or feeling, about the marriage, about his drinking, or about his life. So the therapeutic focus shifted to me and my childhood trauma and its buried abuse.

I worked hard on myself that year, but when the therapist announced that he thought we were done with therapy, we had never broached Mark's drinking. I protested. I wanted to talk about Mark's physical and emotional absence. I wanted to talk about how he no longer wanted to make love unless he was drunk, how he was kind to me only when he was drunk, and was only in a good mood when he was drunk. I wanted to talk about my hurt and despair living with him while living without him. I loved this man. But the therapist insisted we were done and Mark was all too willing to agree with him. So, we stopped.

As Mark's disease progressed, his behavior escalated, and our marriage was falling apart.

Mark drank and flirted with other women, oblivious to me standing beside him. At a neighborhood pool party, hosted by a single mom who also drank heavily, he stayed behind when I left to take Michael home to bed. I sat in a lawn chair on the dark patio until he stumbled home at 3 a.m. I didn't want to know, so I didn't ask.

One fall evening, the police came to the door. It was a Saturday night and Mark was supposed to have been on campus parking cars for the MSU football game. They observed a man weaving and lurching through our front yard. When the police approached him, he insisted that he lived there. They had checked his ID. Mark was standing behind them. Was I okay with letting him in?

"He lives here," I replied, as Mark brushed past me into the house and up the stairs to his bedroom. After thanking and reassuring the police, I headed up the stairs after him. He had passed out, diagonal, across the bed. Having the police at the door, in addition to his other typical alcoholic behaviors, was a final straw. I was so tired.

The next morning, Mark was cheerful. He made pancakes and bacon for breakfast. He set a cup of coffee on the dining room table in front of me saying that breakfast was 'coming right up'.

Setting both our plates down in front of us, he started talking about buying a camper trailer because when we camped on vacation, I was disenchanted with sleeping on the ground, or in a tent in the rain. He went on. I don't remember what he said, or even if I was listening to what he said. I was staring at the pancakes, cold on my plate, when he stopped for a moment and asked me, "What do you think?"

"I don't want to buy a camper," I said, "I want a divorce."

He froze, silently staring at me. I went on.

"I don't want to live with your drinking anymore. You need to make a choice—it's me and our marriage, or it's alcohol. I am 100 percent done with living with a drunk. It's up to you."

And for the next five days, he was sober.

The following Saturday night, after working parking at MSU, he came home so drunk that two of his friends carried him in the back door, his arms around their shoulders, head lolling. When he lifted his head and saw my shock, and my tears, he mumbled how much he loved me. They laid him face down on the kitchen floor and we turned his head to the side in case he threw up.

The next morning, he was still face down. Michael and I stepped over and around him to make our breakfasts.

I was broken. I had been warned by my Al-Anon friends about the 'ultimatum', the demand to stop drinking or the marriage was over. I was warned that I needed to be in the space where if he chose alcohol over me, I could accept his choice. That week, I filed for divorce.

After the divorce, during which we were kinder to each other than we had been in years, Mark got sober. Over the next four years, we attempted repeatedly to put the relationship back together. We talked honestly and made love like newlyweds. He wanted me again; he valued me again—we had some wonderful times and reclaimed the love and respect we hadn't shown each other in decades. It was heady, and we were both hopeful. But as time went on, slowly, we both realized that 'we' simply didn't work. We were no longer the couple who produced shows, we weren't the couple in the bleachers at Michael's high school football games—we had changed. We drifted. We dated other people. We broke up and got back together numerous times. I went off to graduate school and Mark went back to drinking with a new girlfriend, the woman who would become his second wife, Jeanie.

That time, even though we didn't accomplish what we set out to accomplish, those years allowed us the space to know each other in a different way. Our relationship deepened even as we were letting each other go.

We stayed in each other's lives in a deep and abiding friendship. We talked weekly and went to dinner occasionally. I retired from teaching and moved to Detroit to be with my new husband, but drove to Lansing often to see Mark's sets and his shows. Jeanie tolerated my presence in his life, and was even gracious towards me. It was a new chapter.

And then, Mark was diagnosed with cancer, just three months after his and Jeanie's wedding.

For the next six years, Mark and Jeanie battled cancer. He was sick, he was in treatment, he was in remission and then, the cancer was back, round and round. He and I still talked, still saw each other, but less frequently. I visited and did Reiki treatments on him. I came to the hospital once to sit with him to give Jeanie a break. But ultimately there was little I could, or anyone else could do. Finally, the word came: Mark was in hospice. He had days. I didn't feel like I could see him alone. Calling my friend, Anne, she agreed to come with me.

The day we went to see Mark in hospice, he was sitting up in bed, but unresponsive. He was gaunt, his skin shiny and stretched over his skeletal face—he was almost unrecognizable.

As Jeanie and I stood by his bed, she told me the story of driving Mark to University of Michigan Rogel Cancer Center in Ann Arbor two days before, looking for another treatment. His bones were brittle, having been eaten away by the cancer. They told him there was nothing more they could do; he was dying.

A wave of hot pain broke over my heart as I gazed at this man who was about to permanently exit my life. I felt my feet on the floor, heard the soft click of the IV drip, I was there, beside Mark's bed and he was dying.

I touched his thigh and leaned in to kiss him on the cheek. His thigh bone was so brittle, so painful, that when I touched him, he screamed—but silently. Eyes closed, mouth wide open so I could see the white film inside, coating his teeth, coating his tongue— but no sound.

Jeanie came over to stand next to me and I told her, I touched, but I said bumped, like it was an accident, I bumped his leg. She ran to get the nurse who brought a syringe of morphine, which she administered by plunging it into his IV. His face slowly relaxed, his jaw went slack and his head turned to the side. He was out of pain. And now, beyond my reach.

I left the room, went outside and sat on a bench. Bent in half, with my chest on my knees, my face in my hands, I sobbed. Anne put her hand on my back. It was the only gesture of recognition or comfort that I would receive around Mark's death.

After Mark died, I had my second experience with disenfranchised grief—grief without acknowledgement, grief with no place to land.

Dr. Kenneth J. Doka, in his book, *Grief Is a Journey*, describes disenfranchised grief as grief that is outside of societal rules about how we are expected to grieve, how long we are allowed to grieve, and whom we are allowed to grieve. Grieving an ex-spouse is outside of those rules. I found that the people I was closest to didn't want to talk about Mark or my feelings about his death. I had divorced him after all; he caused his cancer by smoking and drinking; didn't you both remarry? I didn't receive a single sympathy card, a 'how are you doing' call, or a casserole. My grief was inconvenient.

There was the question of his memorial. I didn't know what to do, so of course, I googled it: *etiquette for attending your ex-husband's funeral*. The results were disappointing, no matter how many different links I clicked. Apparently, an ex-wife has to have children with the dead guy for her to legitimately attend the funeral.

After much back and forth, and despite how deeply lonely I felt in my devastation, I decided not to go. I thought of Jeanie first. Putting myself in her shoes, I realized that I had been a presence in the background of her marriage to Mark and I didn't want to force her generosity towards me one more time on this momentous occasion. Mark had made a life with her, of which I wasn't a part. She had taken heroic care of him while he was sick, and saw it through. She deserved to be the focus of love and support. I admired her, and though she would never know, my absence was my way of supporting her in her grief.

In addition, I didn't want to hear the judgement of others who had opinions regarding Mark's and my marriage—who thought they knew us from looking at us from the outside—especially during the years that we were trying to find each other again. And I didn't want to defend myself against their judgement of me when they didn't think I belonged there—the side glances, the forced conversations.

So, I did what I already knew to do: I presented as happy, smart and grateful during the day. But at night, I descended into my basement to grieve. The entire process felt like a skyscraper being demolished by implosion—the flashes of light and puffs of smoke of the explosives and then the slow and complete collapse of the structure falling into itself, into the dust and piles of grey rubble that were my heart.

I didn't have a plan; I didn't have a ritual. All that developed over time and as my grief lightened. At first, and for months, I simply cried and repeated his name: Mark, Mark, Mark, Mark. I would lay in bed, holding a pillow, and literally, cry myself to sleep. Raw. Eventually, I got more organized and I began to journal.

When I was on my way to hospice, I wanted to tell Mark how sorry I was. To apologize for the ways in which I had failed our marriage, and him. Since that hadn't happened, I took out my journal and began writing apologies. I dug it all up and wrote it all down. I began having conversations with him on paper. I would write and he would answer in writing. He was sorry too. I hadn't understood.

While I was journaling, I created a Mark altar: the photo he gave me when he first left East Lansing and went back to Boulder, a small perfectly round white stone on which he had written 'Lk. Superior' with a Sharpie, my wedding ring, a Christmas card with green reindeer, glitter on their antlers. Eventually, I added a candle to the altar, more pictures, and a rose quartz tower.

Christopher had retrieved a binder of all the emails that Mark and I had written to each other after the divorce. Mark had printed them out, hole-punched them and saved them. Months after the memorial, Chris called me to meet for coffee and gave the binder to me. During my basement grief, I read through all of them, many times. And I began to feel Mark's presence and hear his voice. I talk to him regularly now, and he answers. Sometimes I can almost feel the shadow of his arms around me.

I can't say how long the process took—a year, two? Or maybe my grief hasn't quite settled, or maybe I'll celebrate it for the rest of my life, but I can say that I discovered the deep river of the soul, that dark place behind my heart where my tears still flow, the depth in my being where Mark still lives, whole and mischievous. Once I was there, in that dark river, I found other inconvenient griefs: Harold, my father, my brother, my Bichon, Gracie, and Aunt Bobbie. And I found forgiveness for those who couldn't understand the impact or show up for me in the face of their deaths. There's grace in that place, love, and a sense of longing.

I haven't moved on; I've moved in.

References

Grief Is a Journey: Finding Your Path Through Loss. Dr. Kenneth J. Doka. Atria Paperback, 2016, pgs. 183 – 196.

The Language of Emotions, What Your Feelings Are Trying to Tell You. Karla McLaren. Sounds True Inc., 2010, pgs. 311 – 326.

My Affirmation

I am safe speaking my truth.

Your Elevation

Know that your grief, no matter what the circumstances, no matter who or what you lost, is legitimate. Own it. Fear its depths and love it anyway.

Talk to everyone who knew your loved one. Tell stories, laugh, cry, all without shame, even if you are not at a memorial or funeral.

Create an altar that honors your loved one. Put a candle on it.

1. Journal your loss: write to your loved one and listen for the response.

2. Have the courage to swim in the deep river of the soul. All the good stuff is there.

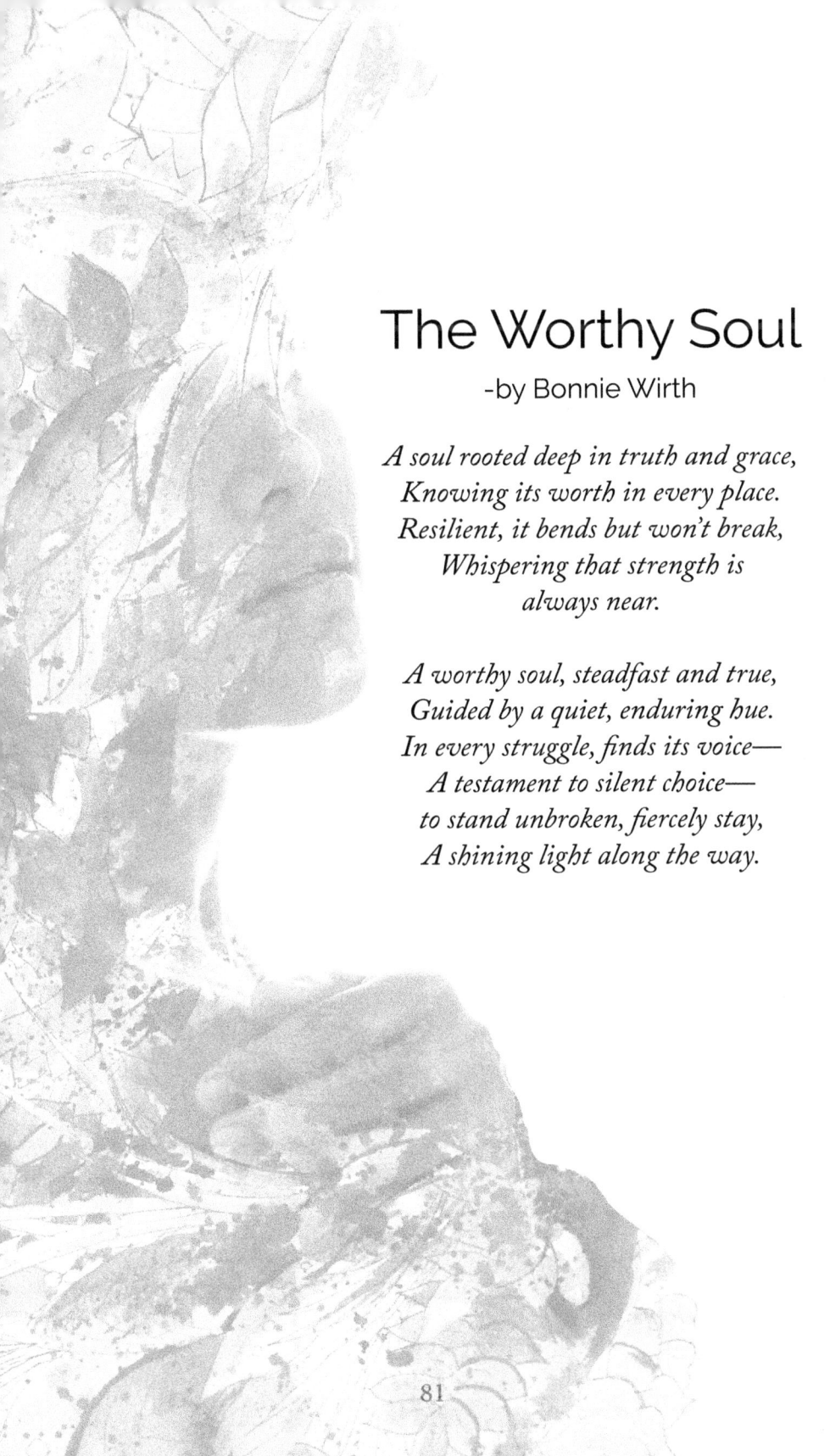

The Worthy Soul

-by Bonnie Wirth

A soul rooted deep in truth and grace,
Knowing its worth in every place.
Resilient, it bends but won't break,
Whispering that strength is
always near.

A worthy soul, steadfast and true,
Guided by a quiet, enduring hue.
In every struggle, finds its voice—
A testament to silent choice—
to stand unbroken, fiercely stay,
A shining light along the way.

MARIANNE LIPSIUS

Marianne is from Cochrane, Alberta, Canada. Not only is she passionate about her work, she walks her talk! Her mission is to inspire women around the globe to create a new paradigm of elevated health, wellness, and vitality.

She has designed an empowering and life-changing approach for women, a GLOW ~ Your Soul Lifestyle ™. It's a unique flair that advances energies of the logical mind, subconscious mind, and the body's consciousness, aligned with the wisdom of one's Higher Self and Universal Mind, plus provokes the physical body to move into healing.

Marianne offers something for every woman who is looking to embody their greatest potential: Lifestyle, Food-Body-Weight, Shifting Perspectives, Sacred Knowledge from the Angelic Realm, or meditations.

Website: mariannepatricia.com

Death Changes

A Catalyst for Self-Refinement

by Marianne Lipsius

Death changes everything, and everyone; how can it not? Although it's unavoidable, it is especially heart-breaking for those who are left to grieve their loss and move forward. And when death occurs unexpectedly, it painfully destroys one's inner and outer worlds, immeasurably, to unimaginable depths that cannot be understood by anyone who is on the other side of the glass wall peering in.

My first intimate experience with death's wake occurred in my early 20s. It was mid-August, 1989, fresh into harvest season when my dad died in a farming accident. Dusk was soon approaching, and we realised he had not been seen for some time. So, I opted to check on things. I casually drove from one location to another, to the various places in the fields where he was last seen or spoken to. It soon became apparent that the timelines of those interactions relative to his field work by late day weren't making sense. With this awareness, I felt sick to my stomach with fear and worry. Trying not to panic, I forcefully pushed my foot down on the accelerator to return home as quickly as I could.

Once I briefed mom that I didn't locate dad, she and I went together. I silently prayed that we would find him casually making his way home. Unfortunately, my prayers were too late; we were too late. He was laying lifeless on the ground with his hat skewed beside him and the farm equipment still running, thundering loudly into the night air, and deafening our cries. It was all too shocking and overwhelming. I was horrified and traumatized beyond my knowing.

Once I reported my dad's death to authorities, I went back home and began informing my siblings. Then, I sat outside numbly trying to absorb what happened and that my dad was gone forever. The night seemed eerily still, and the incessant chirping of crickets was overly loud, agitating my nerves to greater degrees.

As I scanned the yard, I became aware of my dad's dog, Benson. Sensing our tragedy, Benson was howling. His endless cries comprised a very notable and undeniable sadness. Not only had my life drastically changed unexpectedly that night, so had Benson's. We were both left to grieve our respective devastating and personal loss.

I did my best with life'ing following my dad's funeral, returning to work a week later. Back then, I wasn't aware if grief or trauma support was available. I was naive in a lot of ways. Plus, I was conditioned not to seek assistance. Sadly, my own mother was not emotionally available either, or even curious as to whether I needed any kind of support considering what she and I had experienced together.

Living alone in a comfortable apartment on the 3rd floor, I discovered that the nights became particularly unsettling after my dad's passing. Despite being in familiar surroundings, I dreaded going to sleep. It was when night's blackness obscured existence that I felt the most vulnerable, insecure, and unsafe. I would begin to drift off, then awake to what sounded like rodents crawling on the walls. I'd stare at the walls around me and those outside my bedroom window patiently waiting for their shadows. As I did, the room seemed to get smaller and noisier. I remember as a young girl, there was a time when I thought I could hear mice in the mattress of my bed. I don't recall what the underlying fear was then; however, my dad came to my rescue and reassured me there were no mice and that I was safe. And now that he was no longer here to reassure me, insomnia took over. I didn't divulge this to anyone in fear of accusations of being mentally unstable.

I suppressed everything that I felt relative to finding my dad's lifeless body that night, his death, and my grief. Somehow, I found a way to ride the waves of life at the expense of my well-being. With time, the overwhelming fears and insecurities naturally morphed into a new norm.

I was engaged to Hank when my dad died, with plans to be married the following spring, May 1990. It was some time since the funeral when I realised that I didn't want to proceed with our wedding plans. My heart was still heavy with grief, and instead of feeling excited about what was once a promising future, I was numb inside. Hank's view was, because the invitations were already mailed to our guests, it was too late for us to change plans. Due to my inability to persuade him otherwise, I disregarded my inner voice and put my feelings aside.

In the summer of 1991, I was carrying identical twin girls. I just recently crossed into the second trimester of the pregnancy when I became incredibly uncomfortable and had a terrible back ache. I had phoned my doctor and discussed my symptoms. I felt my concerns were dismissed and that she implied I was being over dramatic, which had me questioning myself. Later that afternoon, my water broke and premature labour ensued.

During the peak of rush-hour, we made our way to the hospital that my doctor directed us to. We had just entered admitting and identified ourselves when I was placed onto a stretcher and whisked into an ambulance. We were enroute to a different hospital instead. It happened so rapidly that I felt dizzy and confused by what was taking place. To exacerbate the situation further, the ambulance attendant told me that they weren't going to use the sirens as 'this' was not that kind of emergency. I remember laying there and thinking, "WTF did he expect me to say?" Inside my head I was screaming, "This is an emergency! This is life and death!" My perception now of that moment was that they did not see my babies as little humans; they were "just fetuses". Right or wrong, that's how I feel. Why else would anyone look me in the eye and tell me it is not urgent or important for sirens? Why not just keep your mouth shut? Idiot.

Compounding my distress further, upon arriving at the next hospital, I literally had a nurse yelling in dismay, "What, you don't have an obstetrician?!" My inexperience had me immediately feeling stupid and that I should've known better, and that I had been negligent with my babies' health, my pregnancy, and overall responsibilities as an expectant mother. Labour proceeded although I desperately tried to fight it. Unfortunately, it couldn't be stopped despite my best efforts. Death had its way with me once again. This time, taking two somebody's away from me,

Stephanie and Adelle.

Heart-broken and devastated, I took time with each of my little babes, holding them in my hands, counting their fingers and toes, and looking into their tiny faces, while trying to comprehend what happened. Later that evening, Hank and I held a private service for our girls in the hospital's chapel. I was no longer an expectant mother of identical twins; instead, I was a grieving mother.

I was having trouble sleeping at night once again. This time, I heard my babies' cries. I would scramble awake to soothe them, only to be bitch-slapped by a jolt of reality that they were gone and there wasn't anything I could do for them. And, making my heartbreak even more painful, our neighbors a few houses away were also having twins. Their progressed joy and expanding family made me feel resentful, and even jealous. As much as I liked them, I was angered by them and infuriated with the Universe.

I recall someone encouraging a grief support group, but the truth was, I didn't feel safe sharing such a personal experience with strangers, even though they, too, were there because of a loss. Unfortunately, anytime I attempted to talk about it with Hank, he was blinded by his own grief and anger that it always ended the same way for us each time, nowhere. Gradually it birthed into an elephant within our marriage.

A couple of years later, we were blessed with a son, along with medical care by an attentive doctor throughout my pregnancy. We were judged, even by family, for being over-protective of our son. In some ways, we may have been, but those who judged had not lived through our trauma of losing our first little ones and what that meant to our hearts and our dreams. And they were not there in the mess of our loss helping us to recover either.

The love I held for my baby when he was born was immeasurable; and it still is! Later, when Hank wanted another child, I was apprehensive and even somewhat disinterested. I could not fathom how I could possibly love another child as deeply as I did for our son. Yet, when it comes to matters of the heart, all things are truly possible. We were blessed with another boy who I had instantaneously fell in love with; and still love with all my heart and soul!

Although life appeared to be somewhat breathable for a while, the accumulation of my childhood traumas, my dad's death, and the loss of our identical twin girls took its toll on me in many ways, inconspicuously through my marriage, as a mother, socially, and professionally. I was incredibly unhappy; however, I learned how to be a champion at masking my pain. It was a self-preservation skill I learned as a child. As a result, though, I struggled with perfectionism and low self-esteem. I developed chronic food and body issues. I was terribly insecure and easily intimidated. I conformed to others' expectations, idealisms, needs, etc.… the list goes on and on.

Over time I lost myself as a person, and my sense of self-identity disoriented. I had no voice. I had no dreams. I never had a BFF. Everything I did was for the benefit of others. My wants were minimized to fit into the most compact, tiniest box. I merely existed in life instead of honouring my needs, my truths, and my pain; overall, myself.

Life eventually took a turn for the better after I read, *The Secret*. It captured my attention and had me feeling enthused and motivated. I reflected on e.v.e.r.y.t.h.i.n.g beyond the physical eye. I always felt there was 'something right there' in front of me, practically hitting me in the nose, but I could never really tell what it was. And this book validated that my intuition was on point.

My library card got a workout! The more I read about the universe, quantum field teachings, and alchemy, the more I wanted for myself. I was unaware until then how deprived and parched my soul was in terms of what it yearned for. I was finally doing something for myself that made me feel alive.

Through self-study, I developed the ability to see auras, leading me on a path to explore other possibilities relative to higher realms of consciousness. I felt excited about being able to connect with Light Realms and was inspired and enlightened by the Universal Laws. I was beginning to feel whole. By osmosis, I transitioned from being a practicing Catholic to being deeply spiritual, embodying a refined version of authenticity. I woke to each new day with gratitude, enthusiasm and anticipation, feeling joy for a change. It was like I had my finger on the pulse of something really, really good until…

The fall of 2014, when death came knocking on my door once again; this time Hank died. The days leading to Hank's death and his passing were traumatizing. I was 48 years old when my whole world as I knew it collapsed. Everything shattered into a million plus pieces, no longer fitting together. Those pieces that were once held together by life's elixir of highs and lows, and the experiences in between, no longer contained any whispers of significance. After 24.5 years of being married, I was now a widow and a single parent.

I felt like I had been engulfed by something enormous, chewed up and spit out. It catapulted me to the ground leaving me sprawled out in what felt like familiar surroundings, but from some other life. Kinda familiar, but not.

Hey, what the f* just happened? How did all of 'that' turn into 'this'? I had become a casualty of something massive that had me stumbling blindly, unable to hold myself upright. It left me disoriented, and to my own devices.

My head was numb, my body heavy. I had a pain in my heart that went to unfathomable depths within the crevasses of my being. Everything and everyone I heard sounded muffled and distant, like I was underwater. And I felt like I was suffocating; I could barely breathe. I didn't know how to express what I felt, let alone partake in a strained, casual conversation. I had no interest in small talk. It was too exhausting. And the skill that I once had had evaporated into thin air.

My world, my life, had unexpectedly and abruptly changed. It became foreign to me, and it made no sense at all, along with everyone and everything it contained. It was like being in one dream and then swiftly in another. There was no synergy or gentle transition, the shift between the two was harsh and unforgiving. The sad thing though, it wasn't a dream; it was a living nightmare.

I felt abandoned by the Universe and my husband. I became completely paralyzed with fear, and my sense of spirit was snuffed out. I felt overwhelmed and inadequate to face everything that I was now solely responsible for, including the unknown future for my sons and me.

My cognitive faculties were in a state of disarray, making the simplest of tasks problematic for me. And I felt misplaced in a life that I didn't have a frame of reference for. I was as lost as a person could be. I was barely surviving. I could sit in the same spot that felt like a short while only to discover the day passed by. And when I couldn't sit, I would walk the day away. I didn't know who I was in this world, where I belonged, or how to live this life that was thrust upon me.

The people who I knew socially and professionally, there was now a disconnect between us. I no longer had anything to say or felt like we had anything in common. And truth be told, they no longer knew me. How could they? I didn't even recognize myself. But I get it. That's what we do when shit goes sideways for people. We show up and be there for them. I've done it myself although I had no clue how truly distressing it was for them, until now.

Although I was a shit show in my grief, I did my best to be present for my sons. I know they needed more from me. They deserved better. I either did not know what that was or I didn't know how to do it any differently. It was a matter of one or the other. As much as I felt like I let them down, the one thing I did do right though was that I never abandoned them. I was relentless with offering them grief support. I took their hearts into consideration for every decision I had to make. I talked with them about all that I was faced with and that had to be done. I included them in everything that affected their interests and ours as a family.

I am sincerely grateful for the great friends they had, who came from good-hearted and compassionate families. I can't imagine what would've happened if they didn't have such good, wholesome people by their side.

Our dogs, Oscar and Miah, had their share of tears too. They would lay on the entrance floor with their heads between their front paws and noses to the door, crying, whimpering, and waiting for Hank to come home. Their grief was so apparent. There was even a time when Oscar's cries sounded like human sobbing, so much so that my youngest bolted from his room to console, thinking it was me he heard. How extraordinary it is that in one lifetime two generations have such parallel experiences. My son was grappling with coming to terms with his father's death and hearing the dog's anguish similarly to what I had all those years ago when my dad died.

After the funeral everyone went back to their own lives. That's the cycle, right? That switch of having people around to being alone, however, was extremely difficult for me to adapt to. The house became exceptionally quiet. There were no distractions. No more phone calls. No one at the door. And everything I wanted to avoid blatantly stared me in the face. The worst thing was that I was tremendously uncomfortable with my own company. Unconsciously, this is what drove me to walk endlessly for hours at a time.

There was a brief period in which I did not see anyone. Then, my mom stopped by to check on us. Of course, before she left, she hugged me. That contact of being held by another human touched me so deeply and profoundly. I collapsed in her arms and sobbed from the depths of my soul. I could not stop the flow of tears or hide my deprivation of being held, nor the deep anguish that was suffocating me. I wasn't aware of what I was missing in terms of human contact until that moment. The kind of healing that transpires simply through human touch is incredibly powerful, intrinsic, and transcendent. I realised the value of that from my mom's hug that day and prayed others would not take their loved ones or their hugs for granted. Life's lessons sure show up for us in an assortment of ways, don't they?

I lost my sense of identity. I no longer was married, or 'Mrs.'

It was no longer 'Henry, Marianne and the boys'. The shell of who I knew myself to be no longer fit. I didn't even recognize my own reflection in the mirror. I would observe her briefly, with dull curiosity. She was a stranger to me after all, so I avoided her whenever possible. And I was empty and had nothing to offer her anyway.

I was consumed by fear, had anxiety, depression, and operated on very little sleep. It was when I was just drifting off or only briefly asleep when I would wake to seeing spirit entering my bedroom, standing across the room, by the foot of the bed, or right beside me. Some would reach out to touch me, while others hovered above me. I'm talking full body detail, skin tone and colour, hair texture and colour, colour of fabric, and whether they were girls, women or men. I even apologized when almost bumping into them as I turned over in bed (ha-ha-ha). Occasionally, there was a telepathy of communication that effortlessly transpired between us. These interactions were not restricted to nights either. I would see spirit in my waking hours too, whether I was in the garage, walking in the park, shopping, driving, etc. This happened so frequently that I had to pay close attention to discern which realm I was engaging with.

To acclimatize to my new life, I drank beer or wine to dull my pain, the numbness, and social awkwardness; nothing extreme though. And because I lost sense of my body's cues, it no longer expected food; I could go days without eating much of anything. Nevertheless, it did get to a point when one of my siblings strongly encouraged self-care or they would take some form of action on my behalf. That was a promise I knew would be followed through. So, I began with a small, thinly sliced piece of apple, which took me 6 hours to eat. It reminded me of the days so long ago when I was a young girl and was forced to eat when I wasn't hungry. Eventually, over time, I reintroduced food to my body, regained some sense of appetite, and slowly enticed my body to become healthier.

My doctor sent me back to work only 6-weeks after my husband's passing even though I made it clear that I had a very demanding workload, I still wasn't sleeping, not eating much, and was extremely depressed. I got medication for the depression, time with a psychologist, and ruled back to work. It left me wondering what his expectations would be if it was him who had lost his wife.

Because I was not emotionally, mentally, or physically healthy when I returned to work, I eventually broke down. I was leaving a meeting to retrieve some material from my office when unexpectedly I was unable to breathe and was shaking uncontrollably, my legs were incredibly weak, and the room was spinning. I nearly collapsed. At the time, I did not understand what was happening or why. Clearly, I did not make it back to that meeting and was off work for another couple of weeks to recover.

I returned to my job once again ready to give it my best for the greater good. As it turned out, the clients I was directed to assist were women whose husbands were dying; go figure. Listening to their stories, I provided them with the support and information they needed. Even though my own grief was still fresh on the surface of my heart and my tears wet on my sleeves, I stuffed down my own personal hell along with the heartbreak I sensed for them. I showed up as best as I could; however, I stumbled through the conversations like a dolt, quite frankly. Not my proudest moments, but I had no other choice. It felt like I did a disservice, but really, it was a combination of my doctor and thoughtless assignments which seeded the disservice.

Death changed me professionally. I found it hard to smile, be enthusiastic, or interested in idle chit-chat, although I remained polite and respectful. I no longer had what it took to fight the good fight for others, to be their champion, and have that 'will do right now' attitude. Their problems appeared superficial and trivial compared to the real-life difficulties that I was coping with. I detested high expectations with unrealistic timelines. It was quite easy to call shit out when ego-driven needs superseded the agenda for the greater good. And I had zero tolerance for intimidation tactics or threats by any level of authority; after all, I had already been to hell and back. I stood my ground fearlessly. Apparently, my anger and grief summoned my goddess warrior archetype forward, which was not always welcomed by others, as you can imagine. Yet, I maintained my work ethic with the remaining strength I had within me. I even put in extra hours for priority requests, unpaid at that, when I should have been home with my sons.

The job took its toll on me. I eventually realised I wasn't the right person for it anymore. I had changed too much. It became evident to me that I wasn't willing to compromise my needs any further, not for anyone or for any job. If I learned anything from my husband's death, it was that there is more to life than what a job entails, and I was more important than any job. So, hasta la vista, baby.

In addition to departing from my employment 15-months after the loss of my husband, I made the decision to sell our home. This wasn't easy to share with my sons because it seemed to me, they were just beginning to find their sense of balance, relax into life, and even smile a little. And now, I was responsible for disrupting our family life even more.

I found myself on top of a mountain, quite literally. It was from this vantage point that I not only felt some hope for the future, but I could envision it as well. Ascending Ha Ling was invigorating and it instilled a commitment to not only myself, but to my sons also. I felt compelled to prioritize my health and wellness and strive to make the most of my life.

As I hiked, a kaleidoscope of memories flashed in my mind, reminding me of life's defining moments, the joys, traumas, heartaches, and heartbreaks. And then at some point, I had an epiphany. Through every dark corner in my life, every time life knocked me down to my knees, I found the strength and courage to rise and overcome each obstacle. No matter what path I was on in life, regardless of how dismal or hopeless things were, I always found my way. Now, here I was once again, being provoked to do the same, but this time, with a conscious intention to open my heart and mind to the prospects of experiencing a loving and fulfilling life abundant with positive outcomes.

As I sat on the mountain's saddle looking down at the town far below me, it was in that moment that I knew that I would be okay. Even though this new life without Hank terrified me and intimidated me a great deal, I believed to the very core of my being that everything would work out. I didn't know how, but I had a glimmer of faith that it would. Trekking the mountain transitioned me from hopelessness to faith-filled and feeling a sense of purpose in life once again.

Rising from death's destruction, I discovered my path to health, wellness, and vitality. This involved looking into death's mirror. It reflected the truths of my experiences and although I was ashamed by what I saw about myself, I embraced my humanity with love, compassion, and forgiveness. I created routines and a lifestyle that supported my spirit and my healing journey. I focused on my health, nurtured my mind, became emotionally balanced, and found my ability to dream of better days. I allowed myself to be bathed by nature's essence and took interest in the smallest of life forms that could be seen by the naked eye, whether it was an ant, a tiny fly, or a spider preying in its web. I expanded the faith within myself and with the Universe. I established sacred practices that aligned with my heart and soul. I healed my grief, and faced my fears, which became the catalyst to overcoming anxiety, depression, and sleepless nights. I became mindful of the necessities for holding a harmonious and loving relationship with myself and my body, and those relationships outside of myself. This awareness cultivated the comfort and ease to be alone and appreciate solitude. I took an interest in every passing stranger. I also delved into diverse studies, spiritual, nutritional, metaphysical, and science based. I immersed into countless self-awareness and self-development programs and teachings.

I completely revamped my inner landscape, upgraded my mindset, elevated my mood, attitude and behaviours, improved my communication, changed what I listened to, as well as enhanced my viewing lens and lifestyle. The Universe not only reset my course in life, it delivered a golden opportunity for me to refine who I am and how I was going to show up. I humbly accepted this gift.

My primary focus began with food-body considering this was a categorical theme since childhood, becoming exceptionally intense after being widowed. I studied mind-body eating and felt like the program was designed specifically for me—and about me. Not only was I endorsed as a Mind-Body-Eating Coach, but I simultaneously confronted my life-long issues with food-body as I advanced through the program, and continuing thereafter. I gained a wealth of knowledge about:

- body consciousness,
- what birthed my issues with body image and weight,
- why I resisted my own body,
- why I hated my body and was ashamed of it,
- what made me uncomfortable in my body,
- why I was an emotional eater,
- why I was a chronic dieter,
- why I feared foods,
- why I was a compulsive binge eater,
- how the body becomes a toxic container,
- and of course, identifying triggers relative to traumas.

From there, I certified as a Nutritional Coach, and most recently, as a Fasting Coach. Adopting a fasting lifestyle myself, I have personally experienced not only shedding 13.6 kg (30 lbs) of stubborn menopausal weight that I gained over the last 5-6 years, I was also able to heal other symptoms such as mineral deficiencies, cystic breasts, insulin resistance, inflammation, high cholesterol, asthma, and skin disorders.

My approach to health and wellness is a convergence of everything I have experienced, plus all that I have studied, learned, and researched, from a science perspective, nutritional, and the mystical beyond the logical mind and physical body.

My past to my present is the substance of what has become my mission, to help women rise from the ashes of their painful past, embrace their power, and embody a GLOW~ Your Soul Lifestyle™ .

My programs and services are transformational and empowering. They shift away from society's command and transports one into a new paradigm that aligns with the truth of their heart and soul, all in the spirit of thriving and GLOW~ing from the soul-side out. Whether it is soul-mind or soul-mind-body, I've got it covered.

I feel blessed where I am today, doing what I do, and living genuinely. My life has more meaning and purpose than ever before because I sincerely love myself, appreciate the mystical genius of my body, and embrace my self-importance. And this would not have been possible if the past had not been my reality.

My Affirmation

My affirmation throughout my grief was, "F* the F*ers", relative to everyone who cast judgments through their words, glares, and facial expressions, who ghosted me, who were deceptive with me, and who were abusive to me. Feel free to use it; yet, if you prefer something softer, "*My life; my way.*" is empowering.

Your Elevation

Are you familiar with the saying, "life's a bitch, and then you die"? Well, death's a bitch, and then you live. We rise from death's destruction as a goddess, not a victim; a refined quality who emerges gracefully because of the profound transformation. And the degree to which you have lost will be equivalent to the degree in which death will alter you.

Respect the time necessary to heal from grief's repercussions. Don't listen to others' judgments of how you should live your life, and don't allow fear to have authority over you. Be honest with yourself. Nurture your mindset and emotions. Nourish your body with clean foods. Honor your self-worth. And be your own advocate for what makes you thrive and feel fabulous.

CAROLYN HAMPTON

Carolyn Hampton is an attorney, mom, artist, psychic medium, and energy healer from Los Angeles. Experiencing a childhood marked by severe abuse, she began to lose hope at a very young age. That is, until some divine beings staged a "spiritual intervention" that made her believe in herself and the plan that they have for her in this lifetime. Carolyn learned to rely on the assistance from spirit guides as she grew into adulthood, and throughout her legal career. It was not until much later in life that she began to embrace and develop her spiritual gifts while healing the childhood trauma. Carolyn realized that she has a passion for using her gifts to serve others and that is an essential part of her life purpose.

Website: www.carolynhampton.com

Nothing Gold Can Stay

The Phoenix Path: from the early ashes of childhood trauma to the wings of spiritual service, learning that our greatest wounds become our greatest gifts.

by Carolyn Hampton

Quite suddenly *he* appeared in an electric cloud of blue smoke, with his enormous wings flapping like thunder, his loud, booming voice bouncing off marble floors and sky-high ceilings. He clearly wasn't human—much larger than any man—wearing a suit of armor and carrying a giant sword. My thoughts raced as I realized that this creature was here to speak to me. My imagination has always been vivid, but man, oh man, this was really happening. Cowering in fear, I froze, trying to avoid eye contact. Warmth and kindness radiated from him, along with superhero-level strength.

"Cheer up, my girl! I have such grand plans for you! And at some point, you'll learn that deep down you are a warrior like me!"

If someone made a movie of my life, this would be the opening scene. Picture this: A waif-like six-year-old girl with white-blonde hair, big green eyes, and knobby knees. I'm not being grandiose, it's just that after working in the movie industry for three decades, I naturally think in cinematic terms. What movie genre would this situation be like—Action/Adventure? Dramedy? Who would I cast in each role?

But first, dear Reader, let me rewind and give you the backstory before that cinematically exciting scene unfolds.

The Shadow of Childhood

From an early age I knew being born with intuitive gifts meant living in two worlds—and mostly keeping that secret so you don't sound like a raving lunatic to the "Muggles." (Yes, J.K. Rowling's term fits perfectly for those who don't believe in spirits, angels, psychics, past lives.) Not only do Muggles not believe, but some dismiss or shun people who do. For as far back as I can remember, I often felt as if I had one foot in the spirit realm, with the wisest, comforting, and kind advisors whispering in my ear, and another in the day-to-day human world, trying to fit in. Like ashes scattered on the wind, my childhood was marked by fragmented memories of physical and verbal abuse that later formed the foundation from which I would rise.

When I was four, my parents bought a big house on a hill close to UCLA. I vividly remember the realtor disclosing an accidental death there in the 1940s; specifically, that a young woman fell down the basement stairs and hit her head on the concrete. I couldn't get that story out of my head.

When I turned six, my father insisted I attend the Catholic school next to his favorite church—the setting for many of my earliest experiences with the other side. Dad had converted to Catholicism while in college and was devout. I remember feeling so uncomfortable in my itchy, plaid uniform skirt and white, Peter Pan-collared blouse, too big for my petite, narrow frame. I couldn't wait to take off my uniform the second I got home from school each day.

My first-grade teacher was a stern and terrifying nun, Sister Mary Rose, whose thick Irish brogue was difficult to understand. "It's like she just got off the boat from Ireland," my dad joked. Sister didn't wear a nun's habit, but instead mostly wore turtleneck sweaters and plaid skirts with a gold cross necklace. She was a tiny, pious, round woman who was hot-tempered and loud. I will never forget her red, angry face as she pointed an index finger straight towards the heavens, shrieking "Woe betide ye" at us. I had no idea what that phrase meant but it sounded ominous, cementing my firm belief that God was watching every move I made, ready to condemn any missteps.

At the end of the school year, Sister Mary Rose surprised us with an award for her favorite student—a carved wooden figure of St. Francis of Assisi holding a rabbit next to a fawn. To my complete shock, she gave it to me. Sister probably liked me because I was too scared of her to speak that much. I frequently had my nose in a book, and I definitely was a rule-follower because, as mentioned, God was watching my every move. Still, I couldn't quite fathom that out of 30 rambunctious kids who could barely sit still or tie their shoelaces, Sister thought that I was someone special and worthy of public recognition.

I can still picture that pretty little statue in my mind, but I didn't have it for very long. I proudly showed my mother that statue only to watch her toss it into the trash with disgust. I knew that in her eyes I could never deserve such an honor.

Despite my family's affluence, I learned not to become attached to material things or to expect affection. To the outside world, our lives must have seemed perfect, and I later realized that that was my parents' intention all along: to maintain the *appearance* of a perfect L.A. lifestyle. No one outside of that perfect veneer knew how much the children inside were being mistreated.

What began with simple neglect escalated to bruises and red marks that I tried to hide beneath my school uniforms and designer clothing, and every day I desperately longed to escape. I will save the details of the cruelty I experienced at home for some other time. For parts of my life, I have no memories at all because I now realize I was often dissociating. Some things are certain: no one ever said, "I love you," asked how I was, or gave me any hugs, kisses, or any form of reassurance that everything would be okay. I also learned it was not safe to share any of my experiences, so I kept a lot bottled-up inside.

The Intervention

Like a phoenix that must first be consumed by flames before it can rise, many of my darkest moments preceded my spiritual awakening. Because of what was happening at home, by the first few weeks of first grade, I began to have suicidal thoughts. I formulated a plan and knew what I would write in my note. I was desperately longing for someone in a position of power to tell me that I was special, that I was worthy of love, and that things would eventually be okay. In hindsight, I believe that this is what prompted a group of divine beings to coordinate a "spiritual intervention."

One day, while I was standing on the marble floor of the drafty Catholic church next to my school, Archangel Michael appeared exactly as I described above—so incredibly large and intimidating, with a booming voice, and kind blue eyes. Of course, I was startled and wondered if I were hallucinating. Deep down I knew he was real, and that we had known each other for a very long time. I knew that he always had my best interests at heart. He seemed to show up whenever I was at my lowest to give me a pep talk, telling me he had grand plans for me in this lifetime. Sometimes Michael would steer me away from potentially dangerous situations and I would always heed that advice. Other angels appeared too, but Archangel Michael left the deepest imprint on me.

The intervention didn't stop there. After that, I started experiencing visits from human spirits in my house. The first was the poor wife of British actor David Niven, Primmie, who died in a freak accident at a dinner party in my house two decades before I was born—the very death the realtor had disclosed. Primmie was only 28 years old when she died by falling down the basement stairs. She appeared in my room as an elegant woman in a black evening gown from another era and shimmery clips in her short, blonde hair. I felt her intense sadness at leaving her two young children behind so suddenly. She wasn't scary—she'd pick up my toys and stuffed animals and look at them longingly.

I often had prophetic dreams of events that would unfold at my elementary school the following day and just knew things: a pregnant woman's labor, a friend's appendix bursting, or someone's death. I would see symbols, such as Easter flowers, and knew that person would pass around Easter. My guides explained that there was nothing I could do to change fate, so I kept these premonitions to myself.

Spiritual Guidance: Professional Life

From these early experiences of rising from childhood 'ashes,' my spiritual gifts took on new meaning as I entered my professional life. Flash forward several years, and there's no question that my spirit guides helped me from the beginning of my legal career and guide me to this day. I started out as a litigator working on many high-profile cases for clients like Michael Jackson and Charlie Sheen and always had successful results. My boss took me with him to work at a Hollywood studio when he was offered a senior executive position, and soon I was supervising a high-stakes, month-long, copyright infringement trial in St. Louis, Missouri, over the film, *Twister.*

A man brought suit against Michael Crichton and producers Steven Spielberg, Universal Studios and Warner Bros. claiming that he had submitted his original screenplay to them, and they had copied his material. In my opinion, the two works were vastly different. Further, Michael Crichton was not someone who needed to copy other people's ideas. His powerful brain was filled to the brim with them and the accusation of plagiarism enraged him.

Original counsel was replaced last-minute. When I met the new team on the eve of trial at our St. Louis hotel, the "lead counsel" looked panicked and literally smelled of fear. Oddly, I felt a sense of calm and instinctively knew how we should present this case to the jury. My guides flooded my mind with ideas, and the trial team listened—even though I had only been practicing law for about five years.

Like a phoenix spreading its wings for the first time, I discovered strengths I never knew I possessed. My spirit guides helped me pick the jurors. I could sense the prospective jurors' energy and thoughts during the jury selection process (*voir dire*). Armed with constant guidance from my spirit team, I began to feel like General Ulysses S. Grant, calmly surveying the battlefield and moving my troops accordingly (i.e., adjusting strategies). I definitely transformed into someone new; it felt like the birth of the warrior that Archangel Michael had foretold.

Back home in Los Angeles, senior studio executives were understandably on pins and needles, worried that we would lose as jury trials are notoriously unpredictable. This one was being reported in the press every day. If we lost, millions of dollars were at stake. I made it clear that we should refuse to settle because the claim was baseless, and we were clearly winning. Like fellow soldiers in the trenches, Michael Crichton and I became good friends over that month. We ate all of our meals together and he saw me making key decisions to defend his honor and reputation.

The jury deliberated for barely over an hour before ruling in our favor. We were elated that justice was served. Celebrating back at our hotel, I asked Crichton to sign one of his books for me that day, and this is what he wrote:

For Carolyn Hampton—It would never have happened without you there all the time—you were great! We kept it on course, and we had the outcome we all deserved. With love, Michael Crichton, 29 January 1997, St. Louis, after 'Twister.'

Embracing the Gift

Despite massive supernatural help, as life went on, I began seeing my spiritual gifts as a nuisance. I moved into film marketing and production law and was working long hours with few breaks. Sometimes spirits would literally chase me down a hallway at work, grab me by the elbow, and demand that I relay an important message to their loved ones. And of course, the intended recipients were Muggle friends who didn't know about my gifts! Nights were sleepless because my house was a magnet for spirit activity. I could see what looked like a highway of spirits going back and forth between the bay window in my daughter's room down the hall to the French doors in my room. Along that highway, some would start talking to me, so I would loudly command them to "go away" as I pulled the covers over my head.

The turning point came when I was speaking with my astrologer, Steph Bryden, who recommended that I seek out Bonnie Wirth, a renowned medium in Canada who had an online school for mediumship. I think I am the only person who signed up for Bonnie's introductory course to learn how to turn the spirit world "off," that is, to *not* develop those abilities. When we connected by phone and I told her about my "spirit problem," Bonnie laughed at me in her usual good-natured way. "You know you're a medium, right?" It was my Harry Potter moment where Hagrid says, "You're a wizard, Harry!" And Harry replies, "I'm a what?" I was just as confused as young Harry—how could that label possibly apply to me?

Despite my initial misgivings, I developed into a full blown, certified medium. This not only brought about more peaceful sleep, once I knew how to manage the spirit activity. More importantly, I learned that delivering messages from the other side could be so comforting and healing. And of course, I shed plenty of tears and I was frequently in awe when my classmates connected with my spirit guides, relatives and friends who were on the other side, and shared information that they could not possibly have known.

As I moved through the levels of mediumship school, I was blessed with further healing and close bonds with my soul-sister classmates. We clearly knew each other in previous lives and became incredibly close. By expanding our levels of consciousness, along with the evolution of our abilities, we all reached a level of existence where others, even Muggles, noticed a marked change. The frequent guidance and support from the other side means that our inner world is more peaceful, and we are less reactive to things that occur in the 3D world.

When I was younger, having experienced childhood abuse, I turned into a people-pleasing doormat, always putting everyone's needs before my own, and feeling that my self-worth was tied to other people's perceptions of me. Now, in my favorite stage of life, I believe in myself, love myself, and I know who I am. Finally, I am utterly free from the torment of seeking external validation.

Service and Purpose

By developing my mediumship skills, I discovered how much I enjoy serving others through my gifts, and how service is a critical piece of fulfilling my purpose in this lifetime. Like a phoenix that must share its fire with the world, I realized my experiences—both the ashes of trauma and the wings of spiritual awakening—were meant to help others find their own path to healing.

The work that we do can have a significant and positive effect on others. For example, I reached out to a friend of a friend, "Albert," to see if he would sit for a reading with me so I could practice my skills. Albert was at a crossroads in his life and really wanted some answers. He lived in Europe and was visiting his girlfriend in Los Angeles. The spirits showed me a vision of the two of them walking on Santa Monica beach with the girlfriend walking a little bit in front of him and looking back, smiling, with a halo around her head. Albert told me that that is how they spent their morning, and that he often sees an actual halo around her.

One of Albert's relatives stepped forward to encourage him to move to Los Angeles, not only to be with the girlfriend but also to pursue a particular line of work that Albert had been considering. After that, the spirits showed me a beautiful vision where I saw the couple facing each other inside the trunk of an enormous tree and then tree bark suddenly growing all around them. Albert shared that he and his girlfriend met at a conference which included an excursion to a redwood forest. They stood inside a giant redwood tree that had been hollowed out and it was at that moment that Albert realized that he had feelings for her. Albert was really pleased with the entirety of the reading. It helped him decide to move to LA and change professions.

Not long after Albert's reading, I received a frantic phone call from a friend, "Sue." Her 60-year-old father, "Jack," had gone into the hospital for a relatively minor procedure, became ill, and was unexpectedly dying. I immediately left my office and rushed to the hospital. I felt some trepidation because I had never witnessed a death before.

When I got to the hospital room, I saw that Jack was sedated and clearly struggling for breath, while Sue looked frantic. She regularly consults with mediums and knows that I'm one, so she was happy to have me tune in and give her any information as to what was happening. I held Jack's wrist, took a deep breath, and instantly saw that the entire room buzzed with spirits—like a boisterous surprise party. Jack's spirit was there, outside of his body, looking surprised but joyful to see all the spirits there to greet him. I described the woman who was standing front and center, and clearly the hostess of Jack's party. Sue said that that was her paternal grandmother.

In addition to the human spirits, there were two large, intimidating angels stoically standing guard on each side of the bed. The hospital room was humming with so much electric energy that I felt hot. I began to feel the same sensations that Jack felt in his body—his lungs were filled with fluid and weighed so heavily on his weak heart. I told Sue that it felt very painful. Sue went from telling her father "You can't leave me" to kissing his forehead and telling him that it was okay to go since he was suffering. I felt so proud of her in that difficult moment.

A few hours later, I suddenly felt that the spirits and two angels came in very close and formed a tight-knit circle around Sue's father. Jack's breathing became more labored and eventually stopped. I saw his spirit gently rise out of his body, circle around Sue, brush against her cheek as if leaving a kiss, and then leave through the corner of the room. The two angels and all the spirits were right behind him. In a split second, only Sue and I were left in that hospital room. The temperature instantly plummeted and suddenly we both felt freezing cold.

I was so honored to be asked to be present for someone's transition from this plane to the next, and it was a profound experience that changed me forever. I now know that there is no reason to fear death, and that my beautiful Italian grandmother will be the one to host my "welcome party" someday.

I feel so privileged to have experienced moments like the reading for Albert where I channeled messages from several of his ancestors, or witnessing Jack's death and learning the "secret" of what happens when we pass. To me, this is all part of being a warrior deep down as Archangel Michael predicted when I was six. I am not only a warrior for justice, but also for peace.

The Phoenix Path

I share these stories, dear Reader, to show you that we are all capable of reaching the lowest depths of despair—to the point where life becomes so painful that we might consider drastic actions simply to make the pain stop. And yet, I have learned that if you open yourself up to spiritual guidance—what sometimes feels like literally breaking yourself open—it can take you beyond your wildest dreams.

This is the essence of the phoenix journey: consumed by the flames of our experiences before we rise, transformed and powerful, from the ashes of who we once were. Life never turns out the way we planned, but we can control how we respond to circumstances. As Amanda Gorman writes, "we can still find the light"—we can *be* the light.

My path from the early ashes of childhood trauma to the wings of spiritual service taught me that our greatest wounds become our greatest gifts. It is that extreme sensitivity that makes us vulnerable among certain humans, but also capable of profound connections with the spirit world. The isolation I felt as a child prepared me to walk between worlds as an adult. Darkness gave me the ability to bring light to others.

Rising from the Ashes

I named this chapter *Nothing Gold Can Stay* after one of my favorite Robert Frost poems. It's a reminder of the cyclical nature of life, a *memento mori*, of how quickly things change—and yet, how *change can be good*. Embrace change and surrender to it. Tomorrow is not promised— we never know how much time we have left in this school called Earth—so while we're here, let's not waste another moment.

Like the phoenix, we can transform our deepest pain into our higher purpose. Our scars become our wings. The fire that once threatened to consume us becomes the flame that lights our way forward and illuminates the path for others.

My Affirmation

As Archangel Michael says, is: Rise up and bring the fire!

Your Elevation

Look at yourself in the mirror and repeat the following affirmations:

1. You didn't rise from the ashes to be pleasing or palatable.
2. Your purpose in life is not to make everyone comfortable.
3. You never fit the mold—you broke it.

4. Forget others' expectations—you alone get to decide what to do with this "one wild and precious life" (Mary Oliver).

5. You were always enough, and you were always worthy.

6. You are the new paradigm.

7. You are not meant to stay silent or hidden in the shadows.

8. Your experience and your words have value. Share them.

9. Believe in yourself.

10. Break the cycles of shame and abuse on behalf of previous and future generations.

11. Like the eternal phoenix, you have the power to transform not just yourself, but the world around you.

12. It ends with *you*, and it begins with *you* too!

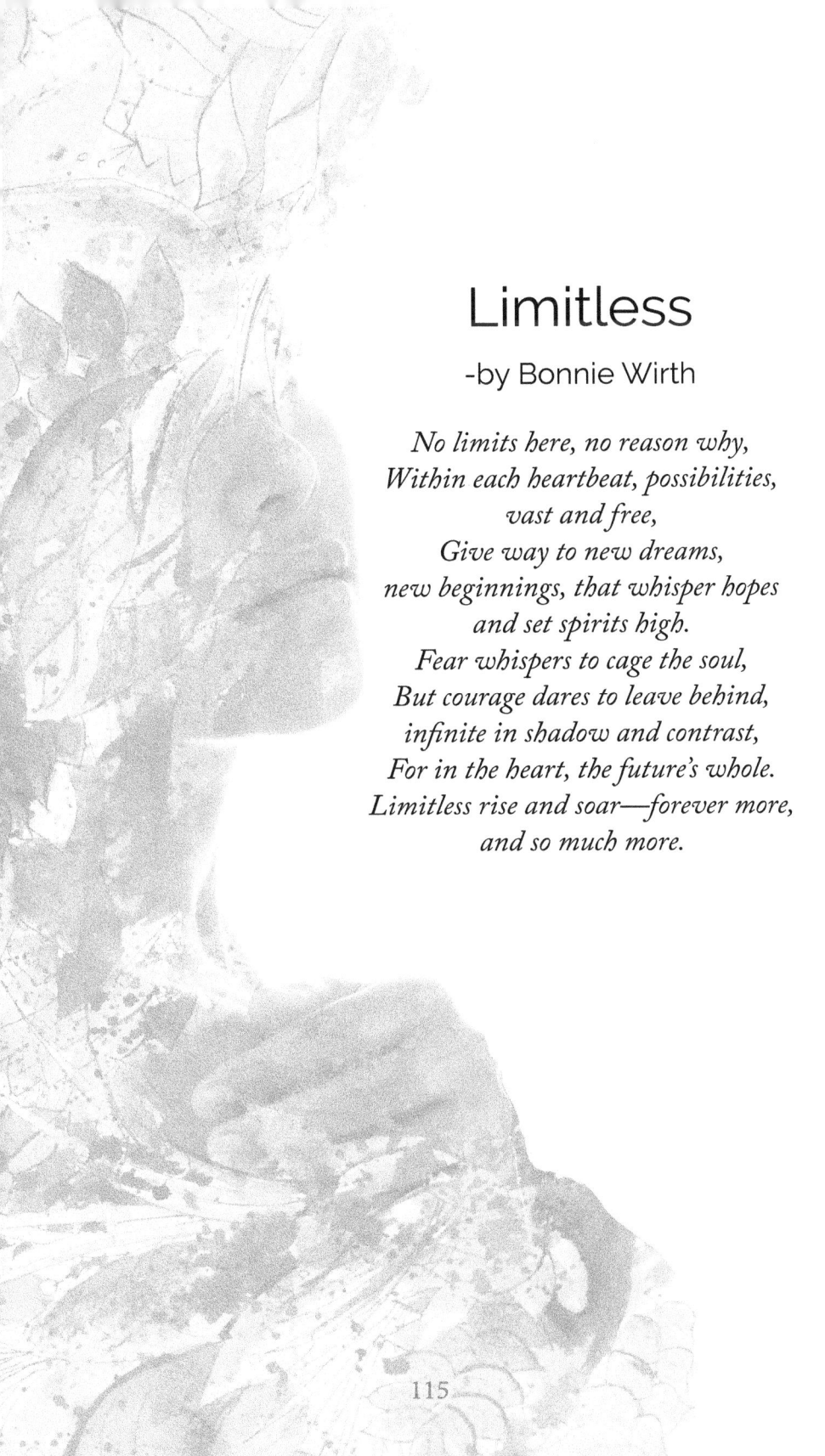

Limitless

-by Bonnie Wirth

No limits here, no reason why,
Within each heartbeat, possibilities,
vast and free,
Give way to new dreams,
new beginnings, that whisper hopes
and set spirits high.
Fear whispers to cage the soul,
But courage dares to leave behind,
infinite in shadow and contrast,
For in the heart, the future's whole.
Limitless rise and soar—forever more,
and so much more.

RITA HERPERGER

Traditionally trained as a Social Worker, Rita noticed that talk therapy/counseling by itself was not effective in helping many of her clients reach the root of their issues, where true healing must begin. Rita started her own healing journey in the middle of her own burn-out and began applying a holistic perspective to her healing, with an unfamiliar focus on spiritual well-being. Pairing her professional counselling with alternative healing ideologies has brought a unique approach to her work—a personalized, holistic approach to healing for her clients. Rita's unwavering belief in the interconnectedness of the mind, body, and spirit as the foundation to overall wellness, super-charges her passion to help all people to be the highest version of themselves.

Website: www.orendahealing.net

Closer to the Heart

Changing Victim of Circumstance to Creator of Circumstance

by Rita Herperger

We all look for healing. In fact, "healing" has become a complex collective goal with the added uncertainty of how it is going to be achieved, or when it is achieved. In my opinion, many believe there is only one way to heal—whatever worked for someone else. I once read a quote by Hugo Simberg: "Some people cannot be cured, but everyone can heal". What appeals to me about this quote is its recognition that healing is holistic, not easily measured, and ultimately a matter of personal choice.

There were times throughout my life when I needed to take a moment and consider my journey with a 360-degree perspective. By this I mean consideration of my past, present and future and how all within those times were collectively shaping my experiences and my beliefs about myself. This required me to question my past, present, and future self. It was spurred by the deep need to shed myself of the "victim mentality" which had kept me shrouded and somewhat hidden from my reality and the full experience of my life. My life was often lacking in enjoyment, and I was unable to explain this situation solely through societal norms or beliefs. After all, I was happily married, financially secure, had two beautiful children, a lovely home, friends, and a career that I chose! Yet, I was so unhappy; everyday was a struggle, and every night a sleepless, restless descent into a vortex of rumination and self-recrimination. Even today as I write this, thinking back to that time, there is heavy darkness that wraps these memories. I like it; this darkness is what holds me to all I have created; it grounds me and keeps me from slipping backward into old habits.

What I share with you through this writing is not about blame, nor is it about gaining sympathy. These reflections are simply to outline how the past is not an indicator of present or future. They are included in providing you with an accurate reference point for understanding my life before I made the decision to pursue happiness, and how taking steps toward healing and establishing control over my circumstances contributed to a greater sense of self-belief and self-worth. I am no longer a victim of circumstance; I am the creator of my circumstance!

The Past

My past is filled with inflicted incidents of child abuse, an abusive, emotionally unavailable mother, domestic violence, violent trauma, a father's alcohol addiction and abuse, parentification, mental health issues, sexual molestation and rape, attempted murder, and bullying.

I am the oldest of five children: eight years older than the youngest. I don't know when I became afraid of my mom; I only know that I have always been afraid of her. My mother was not one that I could count on for any type of support. My earliest memory of her is her hitting me with a wooden spoon when I was about 2 years old because I had left the yard.

Throughout my childhood and to the day I moved out on my own at the age of 17, my memories are filled with, but not limited to, being responsible for my siblings, being punished for chores they had not done, coming home after school to a kitchen full of all-day dishes, which had to be done before my homework. My first memory of this was about when I was 7 years old and the youngest at the time would have been 3 years; mom had tied rags around our mouths while doing dishes because she and dad could not hear the television program they were watching.

Many times, once I was older, I had the added responsibility of making meals for the family and would get slapped or pushed because I had made a mistake. During family mealtimes we kids had to be quiet; there was no conversation around our dinner table. Dad always served himself first. After we had moved out to the farm, we did not eat until dad came in from the field, barn, or wherever…sometimes this meant we did not eat until 10:00 p.m. and still had to get dishes done and get ready for school the next day.

My mom and dad made me and my siblings responsible for their happiness. I'm not saying that there weren't happy times, but this writing is not about how I healed from happy times; it is about how I healed from the trauma of being their daughter and the first born. As the oldest I often felt that I was the one who was responsible for their children, for the house, meals and their happiness.

My mother is one of the most talented women that I know. She is creative, has a beautiful singing voice, and is incredibly artistic. My dad was one of the most skilled carpenters that I had ever met. He built our family homes, and I used to be so proud of the fact that other people contracted him to build their homes, as well. My parents had these beautiful spaces in their lives, but they were either unwilling or incapable of overcoming their own childhood traumas. The intergenerational violence and mental health issues found a new generation; I became a target.

Writing this part of this story is the most difficult even though it is the one that has the most memories. My memories of home are filled with anger, name-calling, yelling, physical, emotional, psychological and verbal abuse, dad's emotional breakdowns and suicidal ideation and witnessing domestic violence—sometimes guns were involved, but most times not. I have very clear memories of being attacked by my mom, hit over the head with a broomstick and blood running through my hair, bruises and pains that made it difficult to walk or sit.

While these memories themselves are a part of my trauma, the ones that still bring me closest to tears are the memories of watching the abuse happen around me in the family. These were daily occurrences; this wasn't something that happened just because dad got drunk or because mom had a bad day. This was daily. I used to dread coming home from school, because I didn't know what I was going to walk into or what new crime I had committed. Interestingly, I have no memory of my dad ever physically assaulting me; he resorted to verbal threats, intimidation and, at times, joining mom in making fun of me. Further, dad never protected me against mom's violent attacks or advocated for me or my safety. He just walked away. In these moments, I knew what it felt like to be betrayed and worthless.

When our family attended a meeting with a child psychologist over my parents' concern for one of my brothers, the psychiatrist voiced to my parents that his main concern was me. My mother proceeded to tell me what the psychiatrist had told her and dad. He told them that I was suicidal. This wasn't anything new to me because I was. I was surprised that somebody could see something that I was trying to keep hidden. My mother, in my belief of her hatred and jealousy of me, told me that "I better not do anything so goddamn stupid". This comment, so clear in my auditory memory, left me feeling intense fear, shame, diminished and extremely hurt.

When I was about 15 or 16 years of age, my mother, in moments of frustration with my lack of motivation to clean up after her or take on her responsibilities, would verbally abuse me with vitriol that even today is cruel and to some degree, unbelievable and horrifying. Really? How can I ever doubt my mother's lack of love, respect, tolerance and protection of me?

I no longer have close relationships with my two brothers even though we are close in age to each other. I have come to realize that a huge part of my estrangement from my brothers was the fact that mom used to very skillfully play us siblings against each other to gain her favor.

My sisters and I remain close. We have supported each other throughout the years in our healing and in our moments of crisis. This wasn't without challenges at times because each of us carried our own scars, open wounds and limiting beliefs that often made it difficult to accept situational choices we needed to make to meet our basic and intrinsic needs. With respect to the five of us, mom and dad believed they needed to treat us all equally. I have come to firmly believe that, in parenting, *equal isn't always fair*, as this trip into my past continues to demonstrate. Looking back, I can clearly see moments when one or more of my siblings may have required more love, understanding, hugs and love, even a monetary gift, that they never received.

As earlier hinted, school was equally difficult. I can look back now and recognize the vulnerability that I carried around me like a cloak and know that other children saw it too. Especially those who were probably in similar situations. I had no friends, and any that I allowed into my life always betrayed me in some way. I learned not to trust, especially girls. I was bullied daily beginning in grade 2 and finally ending in grade 10—eight years of ongoing name-calling, physical attacks, isolation, threats, taunts and sexual disrespect. Suicide was such a peaceful option and very appealing. It's important to note that, at this time, I attended a Catholic school from 1st to 9th grades with daily religion classes.

Once I graduated from high school, I left home immediately. This move was to bring me freedom and safety, but it instead added to the lifetime of guilt and misplaced responsibility already holding space in me. I felt guilty for leaving my siblings and not being around to protect them.

The year I graduated, mom's creativity moved her to open her own business, and I worked in the family business for a few years until moving to Regina, to Toronto and then back home a few years later. It was during these years of independence and freedom that my childhood really began to shape the choices that I was making for myself.

At the age of 17, I was raped by an extended family member. My fear has always been that other people would find out, especially since those I did tell about the rape, told others or advised me to be careful who I told. That is the sum of the help I received. I always believed that this singular event truly affected me the most, as I had not yet joined the dots of my upbringing. I started looking for love in all the wrong places. I started partying hard, drinking and had a few sexual encounters, and was sexually abused many times. *I am in control!*

I had my first suicide attempt. I tried drugs but have such a low tolerance that this was not something that I could do and still have fun. I really saw myself as a victim... not a traumatized victim. Sitting within the identity of victim provided me with a plethora of reasons and excuses for my behavior. There were so many other people to take the blame for how I had turned out.

In the fall of 1985, I met my future husband. Of course, at the time I didn't know that we would be together for 40 years; married 38 years this past June! They always say that a girl will always choose a man just like her father and it seemed for a time that I really had done this. My husband loved to drink and loved to party. He used to be part of the biker environment. There was a small part of me that actually found his dangerousness quite appealing. The larger part of me, however, was very frightened.

Prior to getting married and even accepting his proposal it became clear to me that this wild man was only a wild man when he was drinking. There is where the similarity to my dad begins. When he wasn't drinking, he was also like my dad. He is thoughtful, has a strong work ethic, can be compassionate, is highly intelligent and very loving. It is this latter part of his character that I fell in love with, and it was really hard to deny. For the first four years of our marriage, he continued to drink and so life was very much like it was when I was growing up.

Just after our 2nd wedding anniversary in 1989, my dad, at 50 years old, was killed in a horrific farm accident. I was absolutely gutted. During those two years, I had started to develop a healthier relationship with my dad. This is one of those moments in my life where, when I look back, it changed me forever. My mother's initial reaction to my dad's death was healthy. As those early weeks progressed, though, there were signs that her coping was becoming difficult, which really added to the complexity of our relationship which was not altogether healthy or close. It interrupted my grieving process. Any healthy relationship that I dreamed about having with my mother was effectively destroyed. I was now, in essence, grieving the loss of two parents and was essentially given the responsibility of helping my siblings through their loss, as well.

As I wrote earlier, those first four years of our marriage were very challenging…drinking, partying, fighting, yelling, crying, and my second suicide attempt. Four years into our marriage we had our daughter. I was thrilled and I fell in love with my beautiful baby. My husband's excessive drinking continued and when our baby was 8 months old, I made up my mind that I was no longer going to live like this; I was leaving and was going to raise my baby in a healthy home not in an alcoholic home. My husband had a sense of this as he did put himself into Alcoholics Anonymous and he quit drinking for 25 years.

Our home truly became a very peaceful and loving home. Now, although my husband had made a huge life-change, we were still affected by my own unresolved baggage. I may not have been drinking, but I had no self-esteem, very low sense of self-worth, was extremely judgmental of other people, especially women, and began to remove myself from any life outside our home. I also began to recognize in myself patterns of coping that were extremely unhealthy and so much like my mom's.

When my daughter was only one year old, I gently slapped her because she wouldn't eat what I had prepared for her—I say gently because I wanted to be a different parent than mine were—but I slapped her, so not so different! She didn't cry but looked at me with a very puzzled expression, and I collapsed and cried. I picked myself up off the floor, grabbed the phone and got myself into counseling. Self-love, self-compassion, self-acceptance were words that I had never heard until years later, nor would I have been in a place to truly understand what they meant.

I am not unaware of how difficult it may have been for my husband to live with my insecurities. My insecurities were compounded by the intense, unprocessed grief that I held on to regarding my dad's tragic passing and all the anger and resentment I held in my heart toward my mother.

In 1994, we welcomed into our family a son. My children became my world! One would think that my life would have all gone uphill at this point, but the real truth is I carried a very deep, deep childhood wound, in addition to a not so deep wound of mother's guilt. My beautiful daughter and handsome son, who I could not live my life without, experienced me going through my changes... trying to be a different mother. They and I created the mother that I have become. I really think this is where my belief in the resilience of children comes in, because they are now 34 and 31 years old and have no memory of those first years. Their memories of me as a mother all shine; they're all extremely positive. It truly is hard for me to believe this, because I have memories that bring me, tearfully, to me knees. Once during a session I had with a world-renowned medium, it was shared with me that my children have no hurts or wounds due to my inexperienced mothering. At least that, I could take off the table.

So much of my life had been lived within the judgments of others... judgments which I had come to believe. I truly believed that I was ugly, fat, and stupid. After all, I heard it at home, at school, with pretend friends, and some extended family members. How could they all be wrong?

It was in 1998 that I began to feel an intense discontent with my life. I began to believe there was more for me and so I applied to a university and took a psychology course. While I was doing this, I was also caring for four other children in my home. I surprised myself! I excelled in university—me, who barely made it through high school! I met with an academic counselor who encouraged me in the direction of social work.

I convocated from university in 2003 with a Bachelor's degree in Social Work as well as a certificate in Studies in Violence in the Family. Throughout my academic career, I also gained recognition in an honor society, having achieved academic excellence. All this I achieved through distance education in five different universities within the country, and with the support of my husband. Because of my traumatic childhood, I had my sights set on helping children. I knew that I could never work in child protection, so I chose to work with young offenders. Unfortunately, I was unable, at the time, to secure myself a permanent position. I then chose to apply to the school division where I worked as a school counselor for 12 years.

During my four and a half years of study, I was forced to look at my own life. The subject matter had me in self-analysis and assessment, daily. This was a miracle, as through my research and learning, I also gained healthier coping skills, developed healthier habits regarding my own interpersonal skills, and began to understand self-care, self-love, self-compassion and self-acceptance.

The Present: 2015 to Today

In 2013, I opened my counseling business, finding that I needed some autonomy in my everyday work. This I could do without anyone criticizing or diminishing my achievements. I could also help people within a holistic framework, something that was not promoted or encouraged in my daily job. Up to this point, I always felt that I was not truly helping people, and I realized that I needed to include a way of supporting them in nurturing themselves that really emphasized their spirituality. Then came the wall—What is the measurement of my own holistic well-being? How healthy is my own spirituality and what is it? 2015 is the year that I began to heal, although I had no idea that was what I was doing or that it was something that I needed to do.

In the latter part of the year, I was forced to take a medical leave for mental health reasons. I began my research into spirituality and holism, but didn't know where to search. I turned to my youngest sister, who at the time was already channeling spirit, angels and archangels, working with oracle cards, and developing a meditation practice. I spent two weeks with her at her home. It was during this time she shared her own healing journey, introducing me to what she was using to ignite this process. I wrote down names of authors and other people of influence that she had found helpful: Louise Hay, Dr. Wayne Dyer, Nick Ortner, Collette Baron-Reid, and others. I listened to Hay House Radio; I read Wayne Dyer's books; I began tapping and began daily oracle readings for myself. I learned how to meditate, and most profoundly, I opened myself to my gift of psychic mediumship.

I was doing some pretty amazing stuff, but I could not find my happy. Joy eluded me. After the six weeks leave, I returned to work only to find that nothing had changed. I was changing, but the atmosphere, the toxicity of my work environment was so intense that I could not sustain the sliver of light I was creating in my life. In January 2016, I gave my notice of resignation effective at the end of June. I continued to struggle meeting deadlines and grew tired trying to show I cared about anything work related. I would come home and sleep. I had nothing to give my family. In the middle of February, after a particularly disturbing meeting, I sat at my work computer and made an amendment to my resignation letter—end date, February 28, 2016. I was done and my psychologist friend was right—I was burned out!

March 2016 was the beginning of a new life for me. But did I accept that? No, of course not! I never gave myself any time to heal. I established my counseling business, and over the next few years, I became an Access BARS® practitioner, a Soul Realignment Practitioner, achieved Reiki Master Teacher level and became a YogaKids instructor. Now, I am a professional counselor and an alternative healer! I have always believed that society imposed on me beliefs that unless I was working every day and making money every day, I was not accomplished, valuable or progressive. These societal beliefs killed me! It killed my sense of freedom, my natural and intrinsic instinct to deeply connect with others, and it really did destroy my sense of security and safety. It was all very much a struggle and the wave I was riding on crested onto the shore on which I had previously landed. I had not addressed my burnout and the vicarious trauma and compassion fatigue. Nor had I addressed the trauma of my childhood.

In June of 2016, my husband was insistent that I join him and our two children on a family trip for a couple weeks. I did this begrudgingly, because I truly believed that I needed to maintain the financial level I had given up. I went on this trip, and it is one of the most memorable of our lives! We are very close family and so we often take a yearly trip together. On our return from this trip, I got back to work and realized I really needed to slow it down. If I wanted to maintain the freedom and the joy that I had felt during that time with my family, I had to do things differently. I researched and learned more about healing and what our responsibility is to ourselves in this regard.

Self-care became my new mantra, it became my new priority, and it became what I passed on to all my clients. As I learned so did they! It was during the next few years that I truly learned how important I am, not only to my family and to my clients, but to myself. Through my own healing journey, I found self-compassion, self-love, and self-acceptance. I found these elements of my humanness by learning to and committing myself to living from heart space. I began to challenge many of the self-limiting beliefs I had about myself. I learned about judgment and what it really is. Judgment is a construct through which we develop negative opinions of others based on what they are reflecting on us. We are all reflections of each other, and as such, if I find myself in judgment of someone, it is because they (as a mirror or reflection) are showing something in me that I need to address. When I judge someone, it is not about them; it is about me! This was quite powerful as this new understanding allowed me to shrug off the judgment from others—what others thought, said, whispered and believed about me. I learned how important it is to empower myself with an energy protector: This is not mine; return to sender with love! The opposite of judgment is acceptance!

This knowledge also allowed me to recognize when I was sitting in judgment of others. It was through the learning of judgment that I realized that awareness is our superpower! I love this, because I now have the awareness to recognize when I am in judgment of others and I have the power to change that! So, my self-created belief is: if what I say and do is from heart-space, it is filled with love, kindness, compassion and acceptance. What others think, or how they react or respond is not mine to take on. It really comes down to intent. If my intention is to hurt someone, belittle them, or make myself feel more powerful at their expense, I have duty to humble myself and apologize.

Healing has brought me a sense of peace and contentment, which in turn has brought me closer to the heart. Being closer to the heart means that I found the strength to develop my own relationship with the Divine. After leaving the Catholic Church and all religion behind, I developed a closer and more authentic relationship with Divine Source.

My understanding of judgment allowed me not to take on the opinions and fears of others due to my decision to leave the church. I continue to research and fill my life with theories found in quantum physics, universal laws, and I have learned to care about myself enough to daily strive to maintain and raise my own energetic vibration. I no longer allow anyone to take this from me. I have unwaveringly put many boundaries into place, understanding that my boundaries are teaching people how to treat me and know what I need from them to feel respected. It is from this heart space that I choose, daily, to live my life. Everything I do, say, and think is infused with compassion, kindness and acceptance. Yes, I slip. Yes, I am human. I have found my strength, and I no longer feel lost or scared, nor do I require any outside validation to know my worth as a woman.

Future: Begin today as I mean to go on!

Preparing for the future is knowing that I am co-creating with the universe. I often tell my clients when they are considering change: Begin today as you mean to go on.

One of the things I have chosen to use to help with seeing the direction is by asking myself the "Miracle Question": If I could wake up tomorrow and everything is exactly perfect, what does that look like? Even in the most fanciful of answers is where I find the element of realism. I let my imagination run wild with this! After all, there is nothing in the universe that is not meant for me!

There is a lot that I am experiencing right now, in the present, that I know in my heart I need to let go. It is not always easy as there are some really great and loving present memories attached to what I have. I have experienced dreams in which I have let go of my home. In these dreams, the feelings of loss and grief are great, but I know these dreams are helping me to prepare for something even greater than my little ol' human imagination can create!

Learning to understand the 12 universal laws has helped me to let go of any fear or trepidation I may have for what the future holds for me. These laws also help me to move and think in purposeful direction in the creation of my future. For example, with the Law of Attraction, what I put out is what I get back. So, if I were to consider my future from a perspective of lack, this is what I will create—lack of energy, lack of motivation, lack of money, etc. However, in my awareness of my thoughts, I strike the lack and create from a perspective of I am—I am energy; I am motivation; I am financially secure, and am experiencing abundance in every aspect of my life!

Wow, what a ride! It's been quite the journey and the most wonderful thing about this is that it is not over. There is so much that I can, want and need to accomplish. I have come to understand the power of energy... our words are energy, our thoughts are energy, our actions are energy! I have no idea what the future is going to hold for me, but I do know that the energy of my thoughts, words, and actions is going to shape that future. I am a co-creator of that future, and my past does not belong there.

The only thing that I take with me is the learning that all those moments of crisis and self-doubt granted on me. Beginning today as I mean to go on, means I live my life from a consideration of all I have experienced within the context of the question, "Did this happen *to* me, or did this happen *for* me?" Recognizing this happened *for* me, removes my victimization and shifts me into high power-mode of creation and empowerment to help myself, but most especially to help others. This is my true and soul-full calling!

My Affirmation

I am so much more than anyone told me I could be.

Your Elevation

Thank you from my heart for taking the time to read my story. Some of this may resonate with you, and some of it may not. Regardless, I truly believe that if you can begin to ask yourself, "Did this happen *to* me, or did this happen *for* me?", you will shift into a higher spiritual perspective that allows you to come out of the limitations of ego and pull you into heart-space where you will then be able to draw on the all-knowing aspect of your higher self. This is where the magic happens; this is where true healing is ignited. I send you so many blessings of love, strength and encouragement as you continue your healing journey. Namaste.

BARRIE TUGADE

Barrie's presence and openness remind us of the beauty in the process of becoming. Her words and way of seeing offer a gentle, mutual gift—an invitation to witness the unfolding of many selves, including her own. She speaks the language of astrology—a quiet focus on self, others, and the unseen, the vast and unnamable. Through her reflections, whether spoken, written, or curated moments, Barrie creates spaces that invite wonder and truth without imposing, softly opening doors for growth. Her perspective is a tender prayer, an offering toward possibility and connection. Barrie's gift is a mirror of infinite skies—reminding us that true seeing is a shared act, revealing the boundless potential within us all.

Website: www.kriyaformula.com

Pilar and Posporo

How the Sun and the Moon Navigated Me Home

by Barrie Tugade

I've been told everyone has a story. It is true that I have my share of stories—stories of grief, coming of age, self-awareness. If it involved deep emotions, arduous struggles and unimaginable loss I've got them; but for some unknown reason, all of it has been filed, kept locked and sealed in the past.

Recalling my story feels like searching a word on Google. Expounding on it meant five words like a concise write up on how to install triple A batteries on a gadget. My story becomes referential, with all emotions consumed and digested. This is just how it goes for me. If it happened, it's done. I take full part in the full process, but once submitted it's done. Line up the plus signs and off I go.

But I know I am holding out. There is one more pressing pin inside of me, one that I feel vulnerable to share. One that many times in the past has caused me to be mocked for not having a plan, to be isolated because I saw things differently, to be harshly judged because I used the words GOD and astrology in the same sentence, and to not be taken seriously because I constantly change my mind. It is the one story of how I know what I know. It is the how I got to do things without necessarily preparing or training like a marine to get things done. It is how I say yes with wholehearted certainty before I see the big picture.

It is a story of how I learned the essence of trust through my personal relationship with GOD. It is the story of how this incredible consciousness lights me up and has guided me to intuitively flow through my life. It's my realization that religion is not faith, and that words have the power to inspire or mislead. It's that "in the presence of all that is, there are no words," and that having Faith means recognizing the presence of GOD in all things, in all ways, always. It's that each of us are created as we are meant to be, original vital threads of a grander story. We are all gifted with free will and with it comes the responsibility to discern to activate its power. I learned that my choice is my service, and my service is my currency; what I give is what I receive. This story is inspired by my own experience and when I vertically align my knowing, feeling, and willing I ignite my light within.

Here's the catch. Instead of listing every experience, I am shown an image of a clear illuminated white dot traveling in pitch black landscapes, then blending into vast light. Done. If it were up to me and my fear, my portion of this anthology would be one word in quotation and big bold letters **"YES"**. But, but, but, I wouldn't be able to sleep. I would feel gutted if I bail before the time allotted to experience, if I override the process, or if I don't brave and express as I am guided. So here goes. My instruction is simple. Narrate the story as I hear it. I am told that bits and pieces of this I have experienced and lived. This familiar bit I know to be the green light marker to proceed. It's my GOD's thumbs up assurance that all will be okay.

If you're still with me at this point, then you recognize your "*knowing*" too!!!

Take a moment here. Listen.

Peering my eyes into the dark, my stare attempts to outline my location. Where am I? I wasn't aware I was speaking out loud, when out of no where a voice introduces itself: "You are here." Instinctively, I closed my eyes to see, to heighten my senses. Taking a deep breath, I was summoned to say yes and began to move to locate where the voice was coming from. With my arms extended before me, I obediently let my fingers direct my steps. After a short distance, I was struck by a sudden sense of *knowing*— indicating that the voice was coming from near my feet. I crouched down, curiously running my fingers across the ground and that's when I encountered a small compact portable object.

"What's your name?" I asked.

"My name is Posporo."

I keep my eyes closed in wonder. I feel ease with Posporo.

I lifted Posporo into my hand. It doesn't say much, but the faint rattle inside and its shape bodes safe intentions.

My hands inform me Posporo is rectangular in frame possibly

with a secondary insert. Smooth on its width, yet rough on its length.

"Why are your left and right sides rough?" I asked.

"Oh, that's my striking surface," it replies. I'm not sure what it means, but I sense its purpose about to unfold.

"Why is it rough?"

"To create a spark."

"Hmmm," I replied. Interesting somehow. I know yet I am not clear.

I tinker further and realize that the rectangular insert slides forward and back.

So, I ask, "What do you hold inside your box?"

Posporo replies: "Matchsticks."

While still in darkness, I envisioned the image of slender wooden sticks.

"Matchsticks?" I asked.

Posporo suggests for me to pull one out.

I held Posporo in my left hand. To maintain stability, I positioned my fingers to wrap on its striking surface, my thumb on its left side, my middle and ring finger on the other. With my right hand, I carefully examined my next steps. I placed my thumb at one end and my index finger at the other. This action caused its secondary insert to slide forward and back—out comes a rectangular compartment resembling a drawer, securely holding in place what feels to be the slender wooden sticks I envisioned earlier.

"How many are in there?" I asked.

"Enough for you. Light me up." Posporo suggests.

"How?"

Posporo replies, "Pick a matchstick. Hold it gently between your thumb and index finger. Grip the matchbox firmly with your other hand so it doesn't slip. When you feel it's stable, line the matchstick head (the round tip) onto my striking surface."

I nod my head yes, as if Posporo could see me.

Posporo adds, "Hold the matchstick steady and with even pressure swiftly drag the matchstick head across my striking surface in a single firm motion."

"Okay." I said.

Posporo warns, "Now listen up. The friction will ignite the top of the match producing a small flame. This may startle you. Don't get scared. Make sure to pull your fingers back slightly to avoid being burned by the sudden burst of light. Hold the match upright to keep the flame steady."

"Okay." I replied. I proceeded as Posporo instructed.

The friction between the match head and the striking surface sparked a burst of golden light, quickly dispelling the darkness with a warm, flickering glow. Holding the matchstick upright, I felt an unspoken understanding settle within me—but before I could reflect, I watched the flame slowly dwindle down the length of the matchstick. When the heat reached my fingers, the light snuffed out, bringing me back into darkness.

For a brief moment I recognized the function of my eyes. Though it was still dark, the memory of light lingered and continued to spark my curiosity.

"Wooooooow!" I exclaimed. "What was that?"

I felt Posporo grin.

"Should I try again?" I eagerly asked.

Posporo encouragingly said, "YES."

So I did. This time I focused on the light and how it illuminated the space. I noticed how its glow casted a shadow of the matchstick. It confirmed what I envisioned earlier. I tilted the matchstick to its side and noticed it burned faster, upright steadies its light.

I noticed its spark emitted a smell of work. I recognized how the whole experience was its design. As its glow faded, I lay on my back with Posporo beside me and closed my eyes, embracing the darkness.

"Thank you, Posporo." I whispered.

"You're welcome!" Posporo tenderly replies.

After what seemed like a chapter of recalling what had happened, I was guided by my knowing to wake up and open my eyes. There, in the distance, a prominent circular shape with traces of shadows perfectly framed by calm surrounded by an orchestra of sparkling lights was hanging in the vast expansive never-ending landscape of darkness. From its round shape, a silvery light poured down, illuminating the horizon and a path before me.

My knowing urges me to ask its name. With a breath of yes, I did. "Hi, what is your name?"

Without a sound I hear its voice through my knowing. Its reply emanates from my chest, "My name is the Moon."

With a smile on my face, I answered, "Nice to meet you."

The instant we connected, this feeling inside of me led. I was compelled to get up and walk towards the illuminated path. With Posporo in my pocket and certainty in my chest, I proceeded to follow the lit path. My conversation with the Moon was not over. I looked up and asked, "Where are you?"

Softly the Moon replied, "I am above you and in you."

"I see your light never flickers or goes out like Posporo's matchsticks," I observed.

"That's right," the Moon replied. "My light comes from the Sun."

"From the Sun?" I echoed in surprise.

"Stay on the path," the Moon advised.

"Where are we going?" I asked.

"TRUST," the Moon pointed out.

As I kept walking, my gaze lingered upward, mesmerized by the endless space where the Moon and the dancing sparks hung. The Moon, though following above me, felt as if it was inside of me, as if it knew how I was feeling. Yet the physical distance between us felt like time marked by—past—present—future—separating us enough to know it's both endless and at the same time immediate as in now.

"Keep walking. Movement will help you," the Moon urged.

Following the path I see mysterious shapes and shifting shadows around me. Each silhouette flickers at the edge of my vision similar to Posporo's lit matchstick. Seeing unfamiliar and enigmatic forms I let my feelings fill the gaps and tell me their names through the beat at the center of my chest. I recognized my knowing has a pulse, a heartbeat. As if in conversation, I feel my heartbeat reply to every amplified sound and movement around me. My heartbeat echoes my knowing informing whether to proceed or not. There I was, walking through the path observing the boundaries between what I was feeling, my heart beating and what I was seeing.

I didn't even notice the Moon's light start to fade through the canopy of shadows above me. I found myself in the dark again. Seeing black in front of me, my heartbeat sank to my stomach and doubled in speed, each beat pressingly worried. It was as if I was being chased by those mysterious shadows I just saw, my past trying to race me. Somewhere in between the chase, my knowing made itself known and tells me to breathe. I work on catching my breath. I hear faintly the Moon's echo to trust, but I ignored it. My eyes were glued to the dark and my head was telling me I can outrun the past. I pushed my limbs to go faster. I did not feel the ground shift beneath me; the divots warning me of a concealed a sink hole ahead.

"OUCH!!!" Gravity harshly dropped me on the ground. The impact of the drop vibrated up my legs while the reality of what I was running from feels so distant and unrecognizable. In pain, I found myself in darkness once again. As deep as the fall, sadness matched it in weight settling over me leaving me cold and heavy. My body started to tremble when I felt the insisting bulge on my side and remembered Posporo.

Pulling Posporo out of my pocket, I asked, "How did this happen?"

Posporo thoughtfully replied, "You rushed and ignored the Moon's guidance. Trust is a feeling of knowing beyond what you can comprehend. Trust requires you to steady your body and ground your feet to the present time and space. Trust asks for patience."

"But I felt a panic," justifying what happened.

Posporo observes. "Yes, because you let your eyes direct you without consulting with the rest of your body, without tuning into your heart."

I acknowledged with a nod.

Posporo gently adds, "You even went ahead into the future. You bolted towards it with careless disregard of your surroundings, to which your actions led you here, in this sink hole, with me."

"Ouch, you are right."

"Stay for now," consoles Posporo. "Feeeeeeel, let all your emotions introduce themselves to you. You can even name them. Observe how long you can engage with it. Notice how your body reacts."

Trusting Posporo's guidance, I paid close attention to my emotions and noted how my body reacted. Even though I tried to hold onto a specific emotion, my breathing revealed that I couldn't—I had to exhale and release it. The emotion came and said goodbye. It would be my choice to call it back again, and still my breath reminded me that I could not hang on to it. I had to move. I adapted to the physical discomfort in my bones as my emotions shifted, and eventually, my attention returned to what was happening around me.

A deep, relieving sigh escaped me as I said, "Whew, that was intense."

"What was intense?" asked Posporo.

"All those feelings—the worry, the sadness, and the fear of being alone."

"But you are not alone. You are never alone. I am here," replied Posporo

"You're right," I acknowledged.

I raised Posporo and asked if I could light a match to see where I was.

"Sure, go ahead," came the reply.

I gripped the matchstick between my thumb and index finger, but my nerves got the better of me; I struck it too harshly against the rough surface, causing the head to break off.

"Calm down. Do it again," Posporo whispers. "There, you did it."

I held the burning matchstick upright at arm's length to light up my surroundings. "Wait, what's that?" I asked. Just as I tried to get a closer look, the flame flickered out. So I lit another matchstick. This time I purposely bring it closer to the wall so that I can see what's written before the lights snuffs out.

I saw the words "Karma and Kriya" etched into the weathered stone and hardened dirt wall.

"Did you see that? What do you think it means?" I asked Posporo.

Posporo answered, "What do you want it to mean?"

"I'm not sure," I said.

The Moon advised, "Say aloud the words you saw and pay attention to how each one makes you feel."

Yawning, I admitted, "I feel tired and sleepy—is that what you mean?"

"No," the Moon replied gently. "Speak the words you saw and listen. Notice your heartbeat. Notice how your body responds."

Still yawning, I went with what I was feeling. "Karma feels heavy, like a thud, while kriya feels more like a flow. Karma seems like a result, whereas kriya is the plan of action. Karma feels dark, and kriya feels bright. Does that make sense?"

All I heard before drifting into sleep was the single word, "Trust."

A gust of wind cleared the shadows, making way for the Moon to funnel its light to where I was, with Posporo by my side.

I woke to a rock piercing my neck, surprised to see the Moon in sight.

Drowsily, I whisper to the Moon, "I see you."

With gentle affection, the Moon answers, "Return to your dreams."

With a smile on my face I felt comforted. I trusted the Moon's guidance. I curled my body and turned on my side, closed my eyes and let my entire my body drift in full trust.

I was awakened by the sound of the wind gusting.

Gazing above me, my eyes angled in awe. I watched as the dark horizon shifted to indigo then deep purple; the light weaving itself, turning the sky into a sea of gradient blues. The dancing lights faded in the distance and were no longer visible. The Moon bowed towards the horizon reflecting its silver light and shadows.

"I have questions," I said.

The Moon responded within me, "Keep asking."

"But first, I need to climb out," I answered.

As the light grew, I saw cracks spelling "karma" and "kriya." Tracing them, I felt their meaning—"karma" carved deep into the wall; "kriya" flowing naturally on the surface.

Wondering, I received the answer. "Karma is the consequence of our actions; Kriya is awareness in action."

As my eyes adjust, I watch the sky shift to blue, purple, and pink with clouds filling in the spaces above, while dense ground surrounds me below.

All of a sudden, the ground beneath me began to tremble, causing the stone wall—inscribed with "kriya" and "karma"—to crumble and reveal rocks that I could grip. With Posporo safely tucked in my pocket, I placed my foot on the exposed stones to climb, reaching for a crevice to pull myself upward.

I climbed vertically toward the surface; one step, one grip at a time. Reaching the top, I walked back to look down and see how deep the sink hole was. I was shocked by its depth and amazed I found the strength to climb out of the hole.

I stood still to get my bearings, slowly turning in a full circle and feeling amazed as everything around me lit up—a soft yellow glow like enchanted dust transforming the darkness and revealing the vibrant colors of my surroundings. I took Posporo from my pocket to share the breathtaking view. Though just an object with no eyes or mouth, I felt its warm spirit speaking through me.

"Can you believe all of this?" I asked Posporo.

I feel its resounding "YES".

The Moon was no longer in sight. I followed the traces of yellow to its source. I looked to my right and saw a dazzling orb crowned in bright yellow orange light rising above the horizon. It was three times larger than the Moon, casting no shadows—only rays of golden spectrum shining through.

"Hi, what's your name?" I asked.

"I am the Sun," it responded radiantly.

With warmth, the Sun inquired, "And what is your name?"

Smiling, I replied, "My name is Pilar." I asked what happened to the Moon.

"Don't worry," came the Sun's reply.

The Sun describes their dance. "Each evening, the Moon rises to mark the night, while I rise to mark the morning. My luminous rays serve as a signal to a brand new day." With a nod I understood. "Worry not what was. Be here now. Know," the Sun continued.

"Know." I repeated with clarity.

"Yes, calm your thoughts. I am aware of all your questions," came the response of the Sun.

"I have many," I acknowledged.

"I understand. Take a moment to observe your surroundings. The answers you seek will emerge in time," the Sun affirmed.

"In time I remember when darkness eventually yields to the light. Just as the Moon is succeeded by the Sun," I replied.

"That is correct," confirmed the Sun.

"Just like when all is shrouded in darkness, colors fade; yet with sunlight, they become vibrant and distinct," I said.

"Precisely," responded the Sun.

Tears stream down my face, leaving me crying.

"Why?" asks the Sun.

"I don't know. I feel sad and unworthy," I replied.

"You are worthy!" the Sun assures me. "Can you tell me more about this sadness?" asked the Sun.

"It feels as though my shoulders are weighed down, and my heart is filled with fear," I described.

The Sun's warmth reminds me to be present. "Bring your awareness to your breath. Let your mind align with the rhythm of your heartbeat. Place your right hand over your chest and your left hand on top of it. As your chest rises and falls, let yourself return to this moment."

My body relaxes as I hear leaves rustle and birds chirp, making the day feel like a fresh start.

"That's it!" says the Sun.

The Sun's warmth on my skin reflected my inner light and illuminated the spirit of my knowing.

I was guided to move. My arms circled upward; my body was upright like a tree trunk, casting a straight shadow. With hands interlaced overhead, my palms flipped to release the past, then returned together in prayer, I embraced myself and bowed my head to my heart, trusting what's to come.

I felt an inner and outer harmony. My knowing, willing and feeling all merged into a single vertical truth. This unifying energy seemed to declare, "My life is an appointment, and today's task is simply to live and experience it fully." The force pulsed through me, urging me to embody this wisdom as one would prize gold— to let it embody my will and accept myself as I am. It gave me the courage to take a leap of faith, to trust, and to surrender all outcomes to the ONE that connects everything.

With a resounding "YES" in my heart, I affirmed, "I am ready."

The Sun replied, "Yes, you are."

Curious, I asked, "Where are we going?"

"TRUST," the Sun replied. I was comforted, since the Moon had said the same.

Soft rays exposed the fog ahead. I was in awe of the interaction between the light, warmth, earth and mist in a syncopating rhythm of collaboration.

The Sun encourages me to take a moment. "Organize your day; embrace openness; welcome every experience, and let things unfold naturally. Be patient. Trust your guidance above all."

Walking down the path, I saw broken eggshells and pictured a chick pecking its way out to survive. This motivated me to move forward.

Trusting my guide, I moved through vibrant greens and spectrums of colors. I felt joy. In the distance, I spotted a faint rainbow stretched across smoky grey clouds. I mused how its combination of colors above me reflected where I stood. The wind bent the light to adjust the colors before my eyes. When I tried to look for the Sun, my eyes couldn't see past its glare.

The Sun's glare hurt my eyes, but I knew it was there.

"Step under the shade of a tree and try again," the Sun suggested.

I willfully followed, "Huh, it is easier to see you through darkened shade." Saying that out loud made me ask, "Why is that?"

The Sun magically replied, "Because I am in you as you are in me." Somehow that completely made sense to me.

"Like Posporo," I replied.

"Yes," the Sun agreed.

I watched the Sun's golden rays compliment everything it touched. The Sun offered its vibrance effortlessly, not competing, but simply letting things be seen. I was starting to understand what the Sun and Moon have taught me: that both light and dark exist within me, and these apparent opposites are actually what makes me whole.

"I see mountains ahead," I told the Sun.

My mind paced forward moving faster than my steps, eager to discover what's in the mountain. Just as I caught a glimpse of my bent silhouette on the ground, I hear, "Steady your pace. Don't let what is not before you pull you away of this moment. You are provided for. Stay present," the Sun encouraged.

With an inhale I adjusted my stance upright, then exhaled forward with deliberate steps. I told myself to be patient, to not over think, to trust and let things be until prompted to act.

As I wandered beneath the shaded trees, seeking relief from

the heat, my mind felt calm though my legs grew weary. I soon spotted a dry patch of soil under a tree and decided to sit down and rest. Reaching into my pocket, I brought out Posporo to join me.

Gazing at the landscape, I asked Posporo, "Do you see all of this?"

"I see what you see," he replied.

A gentle breeze provided a welcome coolness. Turning my thoughts skyward, I asked the Sun where we should go next.

The Sun answered, "Head north."

"North?" I echoed. "How will I know which way that is?"

"Turn and face me," said the Sun. "Now, extend your arms out, your left points north, your right points south. At this time of day, you are facing west, where I set; earlier, when you saw me behind you, that was east, where I rise." I followed the Sun's instruction, amazed.

I asked the Sun, "What's in the north?"

The Sun replied, "You'll find out when you arrive."

I noticed my emotions are clear—I don't feel sad, worried, or afraid.

"It's because you are in the present moment," my knowing gently reassures me.

It was time to get up. I brushed dirt off my backside, slipped Posporo into my pocket, and started heading north. Soon, the flat, solid ground gave way to a sloping path of loose gravel, shifting under each step and demanding extra focus to keep my footing steady. With the mountain behind me and the sky seemingly within reach, I realized I was running out of walking space. I'd arrived at the edge of a cliff. What a sight! Water stretched out ahead with sunlight sparkling on its surface, the breeze carrying the perfume of salt, the language of the waves filling the air. In awe I exhaled, "More life."

I sensed the whole purpose was for me to touch the water, but the way down was treacherous and steep. Recognizing fear coming on, my eyes began to tear, my rib cage began to tremble. I summoned my breath to help me calm, but the fear inside of me grew stronger. I could not hold back the tears. I couldn't think straight, I felt my heart drop to my stomach. I kept exhaling until I could steady my inhale and regulate my breath. I paused; I assessed; I asked. I asked my knowing what the best way to go forward was. I waited calmly for its reply when suddenly, a hawk flew overhead, calling out, "Remember your purpose." In that moment I found myself able to breathe with ease.

I stood and headed to the water. I turned my feet south toward the side of the mountain, with my shoulders squared between the cliff and the water. I made my way forward in a zigzag, until I hit an unruly patch and suddenly slipped, landing hard on my bum—"Ooooffff, that was scary!" I said to myself. I sat there for a moment, allowing my emotions to settle, waiting until my breath steadied and calmed. I checked to see if Posporo was okay. When the wind began to whistle, I took it as a sign to get up and keep going. Once again, I reoriented myself toward the mountain and zigzagged down, feeling the ocean breeze grow stronger and the scent of salt intensify. I kept my steps steady until the ground gave way to sand. Then, I ran straight to greet the ocean, where a wave splashed up to welcome me and wrapped my feet in a cool embrace.

I watched as the Sun set in the west, with its glorious orange and brilliant yellow crown dipping into the ocean, and the Moon rose to take its place in the east.

"Head north," beckons the Sun; and "Feel," greets the Moon. My feet steadied themselves on the shifting sand.

"I am here," Posporo assures.

Standing still in the middle of life's orchestra, my knowing speaks silently within me. "There is an order to everything. Everything intertwined at all times." My purpose reveals itself in the present, where past and future meet. I am part of this. And all of this is part of me. I am my own compass. I am home.

My Affirmation

May you notice guidance all around you, knowing that you're never alone.

May you hear wisdom in quiet moments, feeling always supported.

May you remember that your experience are your coordinates to ignite your inner light. Embody your will.

May you have the courage to speak your truth. Trust yourself.

May you remember your name connects you to everyone. You are original.

May you feel empowered to say yes, knowing you belong.

Above all, may you know you are loved and seen.

Your Elevation

You were meant to find these words, as a reminder of your brilliant inner light as constellated above.

Should you feel guided, cast your birth chart. Your birth date and location hold insights on your evolution. Start with the position of your ascendant (rising), sun, and moon—these trinity points are the archetypes of your spirit, body, and mind: knowing, willing, and feeling.

Align these 3 vertically to empower and enlighten your choice.

There will be days when you forget. Look up, stand tall, listen to how the current transits above you are inviting you to experience this cycle of your life.

Ask.

Everything unfolds as it should for our highest evolution.

Our greatest work is to be true to our highest self, to be kind, and to trust our own knowing above all else.

LORI BURRIS

Lori believes there are many paths to wisdom; the light of your inner truth; a divine medicine that creates the wholeness in ourselves and the world around us. Clairvoyance, mediumship, astrology and energy work are some of the tools she uses to support wherever you are in that path of your wisdom.

You may find her in a small town, on a creek in Colorado, USA with a German Shepard and a few hens.

For readings or life coaching you can contact her at: insightsbylori@gmail.com.

Well Color Me OK... and Other Acts of Surrender

by Lori Burris

I wished upon a star
I know exactly who you are
A twinkling light that will become bright
The guiding light for yourself and others
Your wishes so lovely and true
The hopes and dreams to manifest
The Star You Are… becoming the real you
Soul of Light. Bright Star. You are now and always.

Stars twinkle, appearing to dim momentarily. And then they reappear, coming back bright again—our perception of the night sky. All those lights, working together in the darkness. Unafraid to hold hands, those stars know that to be seen again they will need to work within the shadows.

We were born in surrender, completely vulnerable. Trusting someone or something to care for us. Trusting that we will know how to breathe in water and in air. Seeing in the dark. To birthing a feeling of disconnection to source. Letting go of a memory of being complete exactly as we are. That which we are born from and where we will return to. A circular motion. It's why we are OK living on a spinning planet. That is some kind of OK.

Here we are in the dark of the infinite cosmos, kept warm by a faraway star. And we learn to live with all the unknowns and all the fear to… surrender into vulnerability. You know this instinctively. That's how you remember. You know this is your super power— to bring oneness to the earth, to walk and live through the fire, to burn it down, bring the walls down, the protectiveness of the self… back to vulnerability. And surrendering becomes a distant memory. Even if there is an instinctual feeling of "I know this," and yet the idea that in order to be whole, we must be vulnerable to this world—it is in this… where magic happens. It is where we remember our perfection.

The word surrender bugs me...
A lot

Surrender is such a beautiful thought and then you're thrown into the fire of your family. Mine was a hugely brilliant spectacle of alcoholic violence and lies. Lots of "don't tell". And then I became a keeper of my mother's secrets. A place where she could hide herself. Parked all of her shame. Great news for my mom. My child-self thought I was special with this weight. I was a chubby kid. Biggest person in my family. Apparently, I was built to handle the load. It's not so fabulous when you are told to be quiet; or if you do speak it is to lie to the faces of every person in your family (and then some). I worked both sides of that coin. Be quiet and/or use your voice to lie. Never knowing where your feet are to be because the line is always moving. So you're either hiding yourself or hiding the lies. And you become a shame keeper; for yourself as much as for others.

There is a little ego in thinking what a great job you're doing. After you get chosen. You must be special. And you send that little voice that keeps whispering to you that *this is not who you are* to a distant corner. This is the beginning of your journey. The losing of you. A version that you will redefine over and over again.

This quiet, these lies, one day become betrayal by the very person that gave you that special job. You did not understand that the secrets you kept made them vulnerable to you. Their position of power cannot be shared or compromised. Now you experience betrayal. You can apply this to drug dealing. Ask me about that another time. Funny how we repeat what we know even if it looks different. As a teenager and later as an adult, I would sit smoking a cigarette, having drinks with my mom, as I recorded what would not be heard anywhere else. There are still things I will not speak of. The Universe understands my timing, that I am processing that weight, surrendering that, a bit at a time. Using the word, OK.

Some of us are built to hold hands with the dark

The darkness is always chasing the light. If you're reading this, you likely recognize yourself as a soul of light and have accepted that part of our evolution is, quite simply, experiencing pain. Wait, what? You are a being of divine light. That to remember the wholeness of ourselves, that we are one, we experience pain.

It can be physical, spiritual or emotional. I personally am an overachiever and do it all. Sometimes at the same time!

There are no dark souls; only a shadow over our shine

Our shadow does and can sit over the shine of our soul. It's up to us whether we choose to sit in it, buff it off to look at it, peel it off or roll around in it. Or do nothing with it. I have attempted to sit it out. The Universe was unamused; so that didn't last long. The sentence course correction is an understatement in my life.

Oh my shadow…I've buffed it off and looked at it, finding myself lacking in a lot of areas; judging myself in ways I didn't think possible. The good news and the bad news: I have a vivid imagination. The ways in which I can torment myself would make The Inquisition proud.

I remember betraying a confidence (me, the secret keeper… look at me grow) and years later told my friend I was sorry. She looked at me with a shocked expression on her face and said, "You're still carrying that around? OK. You're a bitch! Can we move forward now?" I did move forward, but it's the little shadows like that which become weighty when we carry them around. I am glad for the opportunity to have said sorry and to laugh; and still have a friend 46 years later.

From time to time the shadows on my soul distract me from my shine. They are there to remind me who I am. I've spent a lot of this life figuring out who I am not. And there have been shadows I embraced and were my only friends for a while.

I've peeled off that which no longer served me. I spent a period of time doing quite a lot of drugs and experienced lots of different realities. One day, I decided it was no longer who I was and started my journey back to interact with this reality in a different way. It was a shadow that I earned of great value. I sat in my sorrow, rolled around in my lack until I found my shine again. Walking with your shadow will do that for you.

I had a friend tell me once, "Most people hide their shadow, but when you show up it's like, 'Here, take a look at this!'" He also told me I showed up with about six beings around me and I said it's because I'm hard of hearing. Now I believe they came along for a grand adventure. And I'm still OK.

However, we get to God is how we get to God

If there was only one way to get to God, there would be only one way to get to God.

All our experiences bring us closer to being whole. Regardless of what we judge or how we perceive it. Here's a common perception: Judas was evil, the great bad guy in a book of many stories. Silver took a rap, too. The other part of the story…without Judas there would be no ascension of Christ. Where would we be without that story? And where would I be without my favorite silver hoops on my ears? Exactly where we were meant to be of course. A whole different reality. And there's probably one out there.

An amazing thing happens when you get to experience everything is. Everything is. That everything happens for us, not to us. This is the holiest of holy. The world becomes a brighter place; stars light up in the dark night. Lighting up the shadows. When we begin to look at the evil and the shit of the world with curiosity, we become interested in our purpose. And, with purpose, the view becomes so much more. And we become so much more. And evolution becomes a little less painful. We are able to be far more forgiving to ourselves and others. What is becomes…progress. This light that bends towards itself. This, this is what takes us further and closer to our origin. Our light.

All of our stories, our record keeping, our secrets, our grudges and our slights, hopes and dreams. Stories have been used throughout our existence: written on cave walls, pyramids and parchment. Engraved on headstones and the obituaries printed in newspapers, on billboards and the credits at the end of a film. Scrapbooks and diaries. Our grandmothers. The akashic and our bodies. This is what moves us. Our stories of pain and triumph.

God must really like our stories
because we beget them as fast as we think them.

As a kid I would look at my family and they never made sense to me. Later, I learned all the secrets and complicated histories. Their stories that I was part of…. as I was learning my own. As a child I watched people be angry, the yelling and the violence. The physiological games. Made by the people that were family. I was always confused by their actions.

I thought, "I know who you really are, and it doesn't look like this." So my awareness and what I perceived as reality were at odds in me. I believe this is where I started to work with the power of OK. I know what I'm seeing and it's not matching up… OK. And this becomes… It is. I was learning to be in a flow. Sometimes this looked like keeping my mouth shut or hiding in a closet. I was not always successful with the flow; but I was learning the power of OK.

Remember that game, a lesson in school, one of these things does not belong with the other? That was me. In truth, it all belonged, but I wouldn't figure it out until later. Watching my family stories started my quest, my curiosity for information. The stories my mom whispered to me as the confessional of her reality. Not the visual to the public. In search of what I was seeing and what I was seeing. It led me to become a wanderer of sorts. Physically or in my head. I was off to the races in search of what was really real. What I was looking at or what was I really *looking* at?

My curiosity led me to follow kids home to see their families and how they lived. Guess what? They all looked different. And yet the same. Their light shined through a million personalities, their shadows and their different stories. I would tag along for periods of time and then wander off to see a new story. Even then, in search of what was real. This is still a philosophy I am in touch with as an adult. It's how I listen to people's shadow stories and see their light.

As I started to move through life to create my own story, I realized not all answers happen in a timeframe that I felt *should* be revealing itself. Patience was a virtue that I was challenging.

> The Universe might always have a plan…
> it often felt as if I had misplaced the memo

I discovered that if I inserted the word OK into that moment of challenge, I gained a different perspective. An ability to get into a more present moment. It held off judgement. Or fear. And it seemed to alter time. It gave me the opportunity to expand my patience. OK gave me a moment to move through fear. It's a mindset, a muscle, and it does take time to step into it. It is not automatic; it is an opportunity. OK is a form of acceptance, a surrender to divine will. To flow with more patience than I thought I could achieve.

In my stories, some realities were kinder than others. I will say this: I have found more decent human beings; more light, than not. People showed up, angels showed up and other beings showed up to support my evolution, my story. Adventures in Wandering Towards the Light 101, 2, 3, 4, 5 (and counting).

Embracing one story to tell you in this short chapter of Sad? Happy? Scary? Challenging? They are all worthwhile. And everyone in them—the good, the bad and the evil—I bless them. Every one. The ones that have been and the ones that will come. And if I bless them, then I get to bless myself. For being exactly where I am and who I was in each chapter of my story. My creation story by the choices I made for my evolution.

> You only know what you know when you know it
> And I'm OK with that
> Now. Mostly. Often.

I continue to learn how to take a story into OK and find power in that word. A present moment. A way to temper the challenging of patience. Finding the trust in a divine will that I was in co-creation with. Trusting myself. Surrender was calling and I used OK to get there.

I've always liked to read stories of a reluctant, stubborn but loving on-her-own-terms heroine. I am thrilled when she finds out she is more than she thinks she is; that funny little feeling or voice was far more true than her hurts. She does overcome it, and that it takes pain medicine to get to the other side of things worth it. Better information. Kinder interactions. Far more love than ever imagined. A community that accepts her for who she is. In a story, she learns to accept the dark and the light of herself as a gift.

In the grand research of creating that story for myself, I lived something I've named the zig zag, brick wall approach to life. Ever see that doodle that says "you are here" and what you thought life was supposed to look like and where you are and all loops and curves and ups and downs? That's me! And it's all OK. I was experiencing new ways to contribute to my next story, my next chapter of life.

And I realized throughout it all, I have always known the power of OK. And that it has and is a major theme in the story of my life. Reinventing myself over and over, evolving little by little using that two or four letter word. OK (or okay).

I've been my own heroine, my own story dancing through the darkness. Using OK to surrender myself to whatever path I was on. To get to the really, *real*. The truth of the Light, God, the Universe, the All of All, the I Am.

And it seemed to come down to

OK

a word to move through

from there to here

One minute it's A-HA! And the next you're giving someone a one finger salute as you're driving, feeling less than enlightened. There will be those times when you're human. When you're looking up at the wonderment of the stars in the sky and you don't feel connected. A thought comes of, "What is my purpose? Is this it? This really sucks. People are mean. Animals have a bum deal." OK is tough to come by. All those things are true and also, it's OK. It is exactly as it is, exactly for you. Right here and right now.

Some days it's a stretch. Keep stretching. I'm talking to all the brick wall and non-mosh pit head bangers. I'm talking to the people who get scared. People who think they don't have it. Others, whose stories are so heinous, they think there is no way out past it. You can do it. Your time is your time. You can move through.

OK

A bit of something that helps me get through the wall, or over the wall, or look at the wall, or speak to the wall or figure out the wall or why there is a wall there vexing me. Name a wall, I've got a check mark next to it. I've had people (obviously unsuccessfully) think they were going to kill me. I've had demons appear to challenge me. OK. Yeah, aliens, too. I've had parents who were less than interested to be that, but helped me survive anyways. Despite themselves. Or myself. And finding on the other side of pain, that they were amazing master teachers. After I worked through all my shaming of their parenting skills.

I have a family that is listed in the dictionary and Wikipedia pages describing the word *dysfunctional*. Oh, is yours there, too? The evolutionary wonders that we are is a pretty big club. And my page? I have drank myself into stupors, drugged myself scared, weaved myself into a single mom and a married mom; as well as mommed dogs, cats, chickens, one hamster, one guinea pig and parakeets. I've been a lover, a wife, a tryst, and whooowhoo a jezebel. I've been compassionate. I've been angry. I've been a healer. I've listened. I've not listened.

This is what I do know if you're lucky enough to spin around the sun a few times more than less: you're going to encounter parts of life that we will judge as completely hopeless, shitty, crazy and stuck. There will be bits of beauty. And some of the information will visit you later in your story. Stick around. It's worth it. Yes, I've thought about that, too. Who would miss me? I figured out it would be ME who'd miss me. As Helen Keller would say, "Life is a daring adventure or nothing." And she was buzzing around in the darkness. Every. Day.

OK

Let's get this right out there. I am not Susie Sunshine, living in Cherry Pie World. OK is not about making something fabulous when it is not. As my friend Eileen would say, "That's like putting whipped crème on shit". Nope. We are not doing that… not often, anyways.

This is about OK, this is happening. It's the moment of this IS happening. Even if I'm still figuring out what that IT may be. Taking a moment. Being in a moment.

I am always working in perfection towards the OK. And that perfection is in a continuous process. An evolution. I am more than capable of taking OK into some amazing judgement. This tends to pull me into humor. When I can laugh at myself or a situation, the shift can move me out of fear or anger or confusion. Yep, it's a multiverse in the world of OK.

Bless yourself
You are OK
Even when you're not OK
and that's OK

I started meditation as a student in my 63rd year. I have an active imagination, partly because I was blessed with parents that didn't want to parent. It left me free to move about the cabin in my head and to adventure about the world in person. I have and will always be a traveler physically and mentally. This also presented opportunities to experience... Really? Why? What is the meaning of that? What does that do? Let's call these opportunities. Often in excess and often bringing what I lovingly call "the brick wall syndrome". OK did work in different ways in my life. Is that really wrong? Or bad? Hmmm, let's find out and...blammo. Brick wall. OK. It was one way for me to learn and grow.

I've had great daydreams, nightdreams and everything in between dreams. Now I'm bringing that thought process to my meditation. A new adventure for me. Starting with clear intent. Kidding. Actually, it was a requirement of a class I was taking, otherwise I'm not quite certain how it would have shown up in my life. The thoughts were *"Really?"* I am not a Namaste kind of girl. I went into it with the OK of heavy sarcasm. This class also required a record keeping of sorts by writing in a meditation journal. And I remember the thought of "Uh huh, OK."

This movement of energy, this meditation...came with so many expectations. What will the experience be? What will it look like and where will I go? What is it going to do and what I am going to get out of it? Will I get anything out of it? Brain journey, and yet I knew it was going to be a soul experience. Are we talking about surrender? Again? OK.

My meditation starts with moving energy, expansion and then, hopefully, moving into a meditation space that will provide SOMETHING of interest to me. I like to be interested. Boredom is, well, boring.

I leaned heavily on that cultivated space of OK. To quiet my critic. To appease my fear of failure. To tell the perfectionist it is all perfection, regardless of what does or does not happen. That meditation space became a little intense with OK; because I ended up with so many, in my mind, "weird" experiences during it. And quite frankly, I didn't know what to do with what the moment was bringing. OK ended up being the best way to get me out of my way. To become less judgy and more present. Less judgy. Not no judgy. In the beginning of the meditation, I could feel the energy was different in each of my legs and, OK. Obviously, I was working on balance! I got this. When I moved to my roots, the scene was this: my roots were in a sphere. Cool. They were separate and facing each other, not connected or touching. Picture a couple of octopus (octopi) with their tentacles opposite each other and not touching. Whaaaat? OK. I blew through months of looking at my roots that way. Waiting, until they told me something different. Being OK. Letting them be OK. And one day, when I moved into my meditation to my roots, they came together.

They merged into these huge, beautiful roots. A consciousness that spoke of a oneness. I walked around them, touching them. Appreciating them. Wow. This, this is very OK. It felt like a new beginning. Beyond being. Oneness. As I stood next to my roots, at the trunk, and peered up through the canopy, far far away I could see light. This spoke to me of my place in heaven and earth. And this OK moved me gently into connectedness.

After all that awesomeness, I was cruising that meditation! And then one day I showed up at my roots and watched them burn up and turn to ash. They blew away. Freaked. Me. Out. As I patiently breathed my panicked heart through OK. OK. OK. OK. OK. OK. I watched new roots appear. They were pale to begin with. Somewhat like a peeled avocado seed when you're creating a tree start. And then they became more bark-like. They grew larger, had more depth —as new as they were old. I watched Mother Earth put flowers around them. It felt as if I was receiving a blessing. Could I have popped out of my meditation? Of course. Always a choice. I encourage you to hang in there no matter what the scene is. Tell yourself, "OK." Something interesting always happens. Always. It may be much less unexpected than you think. After all, you dreamed this dream.

A hello and thank you to Mother Earth is as much a moment in meditation as my root connection. Sometimes I call her Earth Mother. She is mostly consistent in who/what she is. Notice the word mostly. This is another place where I often fill in an OK. I generally hug her or put my forehead to hers; hold her hands while thanking her. And then one day a stag shows up. It is huge. Majestic. I do not resist the urge to wrap my arms around its neck and hug onto it; I welcome it. This stag is so much larger than myself that I can feel its breath over my shoulder and onto my back. My heart is bursting, and I breathe in a fullness of light that is bigger than bigness. More than more. A wonderment beyond even my imagination.

After any interactions during meditation, it is in my journal that I work out my imagery. Or conversations. Or any OKs I gave myself to move through a particular moment.

Becoming consistent in my meditation from the least consistent person I know was truly a process in OK. It gave me permission to drift. To see people, places and things. Some quite spectacular, some with volume; some challenging; and some — a little spooky.

It has become a tool to evolve my process; it gave me permission to not understand everything at any given moment. A way to surrender, without surrendering. OK gave me the ability to be with the unknown and the power to change anything in any moment. Even in the middle of receiving information. Some of my meditations turned into parties—my soul star was a busy place for a while. I could even tell you the music that was going on.

I'm happy to report that the party has moved on and I now stand in some amazing, shining light. That light from my soul star is what opens my third eye every morning. The stellar gateway has become much more sacred—my council—the knowledge I receive from pictures or stories or words. I look forward to these interactions every day. And to think I wasn't a meditation girl. The perfection in our resistance is real.

As I kept at my expansion/meditation, things continued to evolve and to change. Sometimes uncomfortably so. And I remembered from that wandering kid, the power of OK. That wisdom has made it easier to step back and observe. It helps me move through fear and confusion and even the nope. Notice I didn't use the term "eliminates". We still, as humans playing out our lessons on planet paradise, for some reason, need pain and fear to shift. I'm not in charge of the not-really-rules. OK?

I find stillness in the movement of my energy

In that moment of my meditation where I move my energy down, up and out is where I find the stillness. The silence without color or sound. A peacefulness that takes me to places where wisdom keepers find me. A silence that has no shame or need for anyone else's story. Unique. Where I am my own.

Another day, another story.… I was hitchhiking (because I was broke and my crazy boyfriend was in jail and I was lonely and wanted out of the literal desert of a place and my soul). Night time and thumb out, I was picked up by a creepy guy (judgy and true). It seemed as if we were in a conversation, and then all of the sudden, we were off the main road and driving down into a very dark, deserted, dry riverbed. There was a moon, just not very full or bright. You cannot miss this definite metaphor for my life at the time.

And just as I was thinking "This might not be such a great idea," some guy pulled up in a pickup truck. In the middle of a dry river bed. In a desert. At a particular time. The perfect time. And this guy from out of nowhere said to the driver, "What are you doing here? You need to leave." Maybe we interrupted his drug deal, or someone being unalived. Who knows? For some reason, the driver of this car said, "OK." Not kidding. He said, "OK."

And we drove back up to the main road. He bought me breakfast at a diner and dropped me off at the place in the road where he originally picked me up. A dark day became lighter.

Angels can show up in all kinds of forms. Dark or light. I have had the good fortune to meet both. It is one of the great mysteries of my life. And I am grateful for it.

My Affirmation

Take a breath. It can all change in a moment with OK.

Your Elevation

When surrender seems too much to ask of yourself, I invite you to find a little grace by using a flashlight called OK.

Our greatness is patiently holding us in the shadows of the dark reaching out to take our hands and gently place a lovely shiny pearl. And I thank the Universe without memos.

Amen

BRENDA GERLING

Brenda Gerling is an International Best-Selling Author, Spiritual Teacher, and Wellness Coach devoted to helping others awaken their inner wisdom and live with greater balance and purpose. Through her heartfelt stories and teachings, she inspires others to honor their own divine guidance and live in alignment with their authentic truth. Rooted in her own journey of healing and spiritual awakening, Brenda shares practical tools and soul-centered practices that nurture the mind, body, and spirit. Her gentle guidance encourages others to release limiting beliefs, cultivate self-love, and remember their divine essence. Through her signature message, *"Treasure your divine wisdom,"* Brenda reminds us that the light, love, and guidance we seek have always been within—and that when we live from that sacred place, life unfolds with greater peace, clarity, and meaning.

Website: www.inspiredwellnessandwisdom.com

Learning to Trust My Inner Compass

A Journey to Discovering My Soul's Truth

by Brenda Gerling

The sun was melting into the ocean as we made our way down the beach. The afternoon horizon filled with stunning shades of tropical red and orange. A small crowd had gathered, and you could feel the excitement of the children as they waited in anticipation. Baby turtles were about to be released into the ocean.

As the sun completed its descent, volunteers stepped forward to share what was about to unfold. Then, very carefully, they tilted the containers, and what happened next was an incredible sight to witness. Hundreds of tiny turtles tumbled onto the cool, damp sand. As soon as they touched the sand, they began to move, their tiny flippers propelling them forward, leaving delicate trails behind them. Each one so small, so fragile, yet filled with purpose.

We all watched in awe as each baby turtle took off towards the water. Every single one of them knew which direction to go—straight toward the water—though they had never been there before. They had never felt the air on their shells or the wet sand beneath them. Their mother wasn't there to guide them, to show them the way. Yet, they knew. Without hesitation, they scurried down the beach toward the waves. And the moment they reached the water, they were swept up and carried away—disappearing into the vastness of the ocean, moving with pure, instinctive knowing.

Later that night, as I sat quietly on the sand, watching the waves roll in and out, I found myself reflecting on the turtle release. In that stillness, I began to understand what I had witnessed. It was wisdom—not something learned, but something born within them. Those tiny turtles weren't just finding their way to the ocean; they were following an inner knowing, a divine intelligence guiding them home. I realized I wasn't simply watching baby turtles—I was witnessing divine wisdom in its purest form. The same sacred force that moves through all life—the way a seed knows how to become a flower, a tree knows to reach toward the sun, and how a human embryo knows how to form a heart that beats and lungs that will one day breathe.

This is the innate intelligence that lives within all creation—the sacred knowing we each carry in our soul. The turtles reminded me of my own divine wisdom, the gentle inner knowing that had always been there, guiding me, even when I couldn't yet see it. By the time I witnessed that turtle release, I had already come to know that divine wisdom within me, but it had taken me almost sixty years to discover it.

As a child it seemed there was so much to learn. Growing up on the farm, the world was like a vast playground waiting to be explored. I loved playing in the garden, climbing trees, and exploring around all the buildings and machinery in the yard. I especially loved playing in my dad's ice fishing shack that he allowed my sister and I to turn into a playhouse in summer. Each day was an adventure, and we spent hours playing and exploring. Everything fascinated me. I was curious and full of wonder, eager to discover what each new day might bring. In my innocence, I simply followed whatever my soul guided me toward, as most children do. I didn't question it; I simply trusted what felt natural and looked like the most fun.

But as the years went by, that trust began to fade. In church I had been taught that I was born with original sin, so I believed that somehow, there was something wrong with me. As I began attending school, my free spirit slowly became restricted. I was expected to sit down, be quiet and do as I was told. With every "no", "you can't", "don't do that", or "be quiet" a part of me began to shrink. I began to question myself and believe that my needs and desires weren't important, that my voice didn't matter. Over time, feelings of self-doubt and unworthiness began to creep in, and my sense of adventure diminished. I became increasingly unsure of myself and was afraid to speak up, make a mistake, or do something wrong.

Even though my light seemed to fade, a small spark remained—a quiet flicker, waiting patiently to be re-kindled. It lit up with excitement when something felt right, but I could also sense a subtle stirring in my gut whenever something felt off—a gentle unease, like a quiet wave of discomfort that would rise from within me. I could sense when words didn't match actions, or when people did things that didn't align with what I felt inside.

It was like my body was my compass gently trying to guide me back toward what was true for me. It spoke through feelings and sensations long before I understood what intuition really was.

For many years, I ignored that inner whisper, trying instead to become who I thought I should be—who the world told me to be. I measured my worth through doing and achieving; always feeling like I had to prove myself. I put a lot of pressure on myself to work hard and do my best, believing that success and approval would help me feel a sense of worthiness. But instead, I found myself caught in a world of comparison where everything felt like a competition. School became a race for the highest grades, the nicest clothes, and the most friends. I longed to belong, so I tried to meet all the unspoken standards, even when it didn't feel true to who I was. Deep down, I knew I was shaping myself into a version of me that wasn't authentic. At school, individuality was rarely celebrated. We were all expected to learn the same lessons in the same way and deliver the same results, leaving little room for the quiet, inner wisdom that was trying to guide me.

As an adult, I worked tirelessly to be the best wife, mother and teacher I could be. I poured myself into each role, believing that giving my all—and then some—would prove my worth. I became the ultimate people pleaser, constantly doing for everyone else while quietly neglecting my own needs. I made myself available to anyone who needed me. If my kids needed me, I was there. If my husband needed help, I was there. If a volunteer was needed, they could always count on me. I kept saying "yes" even when I was running on empty. I craved approval—that sense of being needed— as proof of my worthiness. I thought if I did enough, gave enough, and achieved enough, maybe I would finally feel good enough.

I was overcompensating, trying to fill an emptiness that no amount of doing could ever satisfy. Did I really need to be on the Parish Council, the Home and School Association, teach Children's Liturgy on Sundays, serve as president of the Figure Skating Club, and sew half the costumes for the skating carnival, all while raising four children, helping my husband on the farm, and working as a substitute teacher? The busyness I had created had silenced my inner knowing, but that quiet voice within was beginning to awaken—and it was becoming increasingly hard to ignore.

It started as a whisper. During rare moments of stillness, a gentle nudge began reminding me that something wasn't right; that there was more to life than endless doing. It spoke in quiet thoughts and subtle feelings, stirring a knowing deep within me that life wasn't meant to be so rushed and busy. I began to sense that there was another way, one that felt more peaceful and balanced.

As I started to pay closer attention to this inner voice, questions began to arise within me: *Who am I and why am I here? What is the true purpose of life?*

In time, answers began to reveal themselves. I was getting glimpses of what felt like truth—sacred truths—buried beneath years of self-doubt, people pleasing and over giving. I began to see that I am much more than the things I achieve or the roles I play. Something within me was awakening, and I was beginning to feel that my soul was here for a greater purpose.

As I followed this inner pull, I began discovering new teachings and spiritual concepts that were unlike anything I had been taught before. I was beginning to see that my worth wasn't something to be earned, but something I was born with. This realization became the catalyst that changed everything. I no longer needed constant validation from others. Instead, I started to trust the quiet wisdom within me—the same inner knowing I had ignored for so long. As this awareness deepened, I began stepping away from anything that no longer felt aligned. I said "no" more often, and as my children grew older, I released many of the responsibilities that had once defined me. I stopped volunteering for everything and eventually stepped away from teaching altogether. With each decision, a sense of relief came over me, and I felt more aligned with who I truly was and what genuinely mattered to me.

As peace and clarity returned, I knew my greatest challenge still lay ahead. As the voice of my soul grew louder, the more I began to question long-held beliefs, especially those tied to the church I had grown up in. *Was I really born unworthy? If God is love, why does He judge us?*

As a child, I had attended church every Sunday, and although I loved being there—the feeling of sacredness, the music, the community—I often felt confused by the mixed messages I heard. Some teachings spoke of love and compassion, while others stirred fear and judgment. Even then, a quiet part of me wondered how both could exist at the same time.

As a young adult, I stopped attending church for a time. It had lost its meaning, and life's new freedoms felt more exciting than the repetition of rituals that no longer spoke to my heart. But when I married and had children, I returned. Everyone in my community was raising their families in the church, and I wanted to do what seemed right—to give my children the same foundation I had been given. So, despite the lingering doubts and the quiet unease within me, I went back, even when parts of it still didn't feel aligned with what my spirit was beginning to understand as truth.

For most of my life, I had tried to make sense of certain teachings that never quite resonated with me, but I pushed the discomfort aside out of fear, guilt, and a desire to belong. The conflict between my inner knowing and the teachings I heard each week grew harder to ignore. What once brought comfort now stirred discomfort. I found myself questioning not out of disrespect, but out of a soulful longing for deeper truth.

Those teachings began to feel restrictive, creating tension between what I had been taught to believe and what my spirit felt was true. The new teachings I had been drawn to spoke of oneness, compassion, and love, rather than sin, separation, and fear. These new teachings felt deeply familiar, as if they had been waiting for me to remember them all along. Yet embracing them meant facing not only my own doubts, but the potential judgment of others. It was the beginning of a spiritual unraveling—one that would dismantle much of what I thought I knew and lead me to an even greater awakening.

Being born with original sin was one of the teachings that troubled me the most. I could never understand how an innocent, precious baby could be born already flawed or in need of redemption. If we were all children of God, created in divine love, then how could we also be born "damaged"? Each Sunday, when we recited the words, "*Lord, I am not worthy to receive you,*" I felt a deep ache inside. Why was I not worthy? What would ever make me worthy enough to receive God's love? As a child, I took these words to heart, believing there must be something wrong with me—that somehow, I wasn't good enough, pure enough, or holy enough to be loved as I was. It created a quiet but constant tension between what I was told and what I instinctively felt within.

Deep down, my inner compass whispered that something was missing from this story—that God could never see His children as unworthy. That whisper stayed with me, even when I didn't yet have the clarity or courage to follow it and my feelings of discontent continued to grow. I kept attending church because that's what I had always done—it was familiar and what was expected—but a quiet sadness began to stir within me. The words and rituals no longer held the same meaning, and I often found myself going through the motions, longing for something deeper.

Then, a new young priest came to our parish, and something shifted. He had a remarkable gift—the ability to take the gospel readings each week and make them come alive, relating them to experiences of everyday life. For the first time in a long while, the teachings felt more relevant. His messages touched something inside me. I found myself eager to attend church again, curious about what he would share next. His sermons sparked meaningful conversations with our teenage children on the drive home, and for a while, my faith felt renewed. Inspired by this sense of connection, I became more involved—reading at Mass, teaching Children's Liturgy, and even joining the Parish Council. I wanted to be part of the positive change I felt within our community. Yet, even as my outer involvement deepened, the quiet questions within my heart remained. Something still didn't feel completely settled, as though my soul knew there was more to discover, more to remember.

Fortunately for us, this young priest remained in our parish for many years, and during that time my family—and the entire community—gained so much. His teachings brought light and meaning to the gospels in a way that touched my heart; yet, despite all his wisdom and my renewed sense of faith, the quiet restlessness within me began to stir again. Over time, my unease resurfaced, and I noticed myself questioning even more of the church's teachings. The sermons that once inspired me began to awaken deeper questions. One Sunday, as I sat in the pew listening, I caught myself thinking, "*These teachings must be true. They've lasted for over two thousand years. They wouldn't have lasted this long if they weren't true.*" But even as I repeated those words in my mind, something deep within me hesitated. I realized I was being challenged to examine not just the church's teachings, but the entire foundation of my own beliefs—the ones inherited from family, community, and tradition. This made me extremely uncomfortable, yet my inner compass was pointing me toward something bigger—something that felt more authentic and truer for me.

Once again, I felt torn between two worlds: the outer world I continued to participate in each day, and the inner world that was awakening with clarity and conviction. The call growing within me was no longer about trying to understand doctrine; it was about understanding *myself*. Who was I beneath all the conditioning and why was I here? What was the truth my soul was longing to remember?

Around this time, I was introduced to new spiritual concepts by incredible teachers like Wayne Dyer, Louise Hay, Neale Donald Walsch, Gary Zukav, and many others. Their words stirred something deep within me. These new teachings introduced me to the concept of a God who was unconditionally loving—not distant or judgmental, but a gentle, ever-present force of love that existed within and around all of creation. This was a radical shift from the image of God I had grown up with—a God that I feared, one who judged, punished, and kept score.

As I opened my heart to this new understanding, something within me began to heal. For the first time, I felt safe in the presence of this loving God and no longer felt like I needed to earn love or prove my worthiness. Instead, I began to sense that God was the very essence of goodness itself. It felt as if I was remembering something my soul had always known but I had long forgotten.

Another radical new teaching came to me from the book *Original Blessing* by Matthew Fox. It explained that I was not born with original sin, but instead I had been born with original blessing, which could also be called "*original goodness*" or "*original grace*" or "*original wisdom*". It felt as though a weight that I hadn't realized I was carrying had finally been lifted. I knew that I did not come into this world stained with original sin, but that I had been blessed with goodness, grace and wisdom.

As I began weaving these new teachings into my daily life, I was surprised by how liberated I began to feel. I felt lighter, freer and more at peace than I had in years. I was gaining the deeper understanding my soul had been longing for and, as these truths began to take root within me, change began to naturally unfold from the inside out. I was learning to trust myself again and pay closer attention to the divine wisdom guiding me.

By now our young priest had moved on, and I was once again finding it increasingly difficult to attend church on Sundays. Part of me felt an obligation to go because it was what I had always done, what was expected of me and I worried about what others might think if I stopped attending. Yet, each time I walked through those doors, a feeling of unease rose within me—a knot in my stomach and a tightness in my chest. I was feeling the same restrictions I had felt as a young student: "*Don't follow that path; this is the path you must follow.*" But this time, the voice within me was stronger. My inner compass had become very loud, gently but firmly showing me a different way—one guided not by fear or obligation, but by the quiet truth of my soul.

This voice had guided me towards developing my own personal relationship with God, and I didn't feel the need to go to church anymore. I could no longer pray that I was unworthy, because I now knew that I was. I no longer wanted to participate in rituals that felt empty to me. Then one Sunday our new priest said, "*You have to come to church, because that is the only place you will find God.*" I felt my whole body tense and wanted to shout, "*NO! NO! NO! God is not just in this building! This is not the only place to find God!*" I had come to know God as the good in everything, and I was finding this loving presence everyday within and around me. I saw and felt God in the spectacular beauty of nature, in the kindness of strangers and in everyday moments of joy and laughter. I was witnessing God in the beautiful souls of my grandchildren and in the kindness of my own words and actions.

This was around the time my youngest left home and I had stepped away from all my commitments allowing for more time and space to go deeper into my search for answers. I created a beautiful sacred space in my home where I went each morning to pray, meditate, read, and write. I sat in silence each day posing my questions, knowing the answers would be provided. I was communing with God daily by going within, which is exactly what Jesus was trying to teach us when he stated, "*…when thou prayest, enter into thy closet, and when thou hast shut thy door, pray to thy Father which is in secret…*" (Matthew 6:6) He was inviting us to find a quiet place alone, sit in silence and talk to God, which is where I was going every day.

In my search for deeper meaning, I was guided to explore the Lost Gospels and many other ancient spiritual texts. Exploring these new teachings and committing to my new daily rituals completely transformed my perspective and further ignited that spark within me and my insatiable desire to learn kept guiding me forward toward deeper understanding. As I sat in silence each day and began having my own conversations with God, I started posing even bigger questions. I wanted to know what Jesus meant when he said, *"the kingdom of God is within you"* (Luke 17:21), *"you are the light of the world"* (Matthew 5:14) and *"even the least among you will do all that I have done, and greater things"*. (John 14:12) This must mean that there is something sacred and divine within me, and I wanted to know what that was, because it had been buried deep under feelings of unworthiness most of my life.

Incredible insights and wisdom kept coming forward as I was led down a path that would reveal the truth of who I am and why I am here. As I came to understand that I am *"the temple of God"* (1 Corinthians 3:16), I began to embrace my self-care and made more time for the things that truly nourished and honored my mind, body, spirit, and inner wisdom.

I was silencing the noise from the outside world and going inward, listening to the quiet whispers of my heart and soul. The more I listened, the clearer the messages became, bringing even greater insights, clarity and peace. My heart felt open, my spirit lighter, and my mind more at ease. I had renewed energy and enthusiasm for life, and everything around me began to feel more meaningful.

Teachers, books, and practices continued to appear at just the right time, each answering my questions and expanding my understanding. It felt as though the universe itself was conspiring to guide me forward—placing before me exactly what my soul was ready to receive.

One of the most profound teachings I was guided to is found in the *Gospel of Thomas, verse 70*, where Jesus said, *"If you bring forth what is within you, what you bring forth will save you. If you do not bring forth what is within you, what you do not bring forth will destroy you.*" I came to realize that he was referring to that innate wisdom and divine potential we are all born with—the sacred essence that Jesus called "*the kingdom of God within.*" Jesus was not only reminding us of the infinite potential within us—he was inviting us to express it fully, to let our inner light come forth and transform our lives from the inside out.

As these teachings took root deep within me, I shifted from merely believing that I carried divine potential to *knowing* it as truth. I now recognize that God expresses through me as I allow my light to shine and stand fully in my truth. When I follow my inner guidance and surrender to the divine flow, I realize that my potential is truly limitless because "*with God, all things are possible.*" (Matthew 19:26)

I know now that this sacred, divine part of me is the true essence of who I am, who I always have been, even during times when I believed I was a sinner. It is the eternal, unchanging part of me that exists beyond my circumstances and the roles I play in life—the part of me that always has been whole, worthy and complete. This divine essence is the very life force of God flowing through me into the world, just as a ray of sunshine comes forth from the sun and shines down upon the earth. The sun is always shining, even on cloudy days, just as God has always been there, waiting to shine through me, even when I was filled with doubt and fear. When I finally embraced this divine truth within me, the clouds began to part, and my light could shine freely, allowing me to embody the wisdom coming forward from within.

As I began to follow my soul's guidance, doors opened that I never could have imagined. I was led to conferences, retreats, and classes, and even began working with an empowerment coach.

Each experience expanded my awareness and deepened my understanding. Though it often required me to step far beyond my comfort zone, I trusted the inner voice that kept guiding me forward. Looking back, I can see how perfectly everything unfolded once I stopped resisting and allowed myself to be led.

For most of my life, fear and feelings of unworthiness had kept me small. I had unknowingly suppressed my inner truth and ignored the gifts that were waiting to be expressed. I had allowed my limiting beliefs and conditioning to bury the potential that I've always had within me, leading to self-doubt, resentment, and a sense of emptiness in my life. Those old beliefs and societal expectations had dimmed my light and silenced my intuition. But remembering my divine connection changed everything. I can no longer walk a path shaped by others' expectations. My soul is guiding me to create my own path—one that may not always be understood by others, but feels right for me.

I now approach my life from a state of *being* rather than *doing*. By becoming more present and allowing my sacred connection to remain open, I've discovered that wisdom naturally flows through me. When challenges arise, I no longer fear them. I turn inward, knowing I can trust the divine wisdom within to guide me through. My resilience comes from this connection—from honoring what is true for me, and allowing God's wisdom to express through me, no matter what the world expects.

Now, I live with a deep sense of faith in what's possible. I know that my potential is limitless, and I look forward to witnessing what continues to unfold. My hope is that others, too, will awaken to the divine potential within themselves, for I truly believe the world would be transformed if we were all taught to honor that sacred connection to the divine within.

That night on the beach, as I watched in awe as wave after wave carried those baby turtles out into the ocean, I witnessed the pure embodiment of divine wisdom—the same sacred wisdom that lives within all of us.

In that moment, a deep peace washed over me. I knew that, just like the turtles, I have everything within me to swim, to move forward with faith, to trust the currents of life, and to find my own way.

My Affirmation

Everything I need is already within me.

Your Elevation

Take time each day to pause and connect with the still, wise voice within. Find a quiet space where you can sit comfortably.

Close your eyes, place your hands over your heart. Take a few slow, deep breaths, allowing your body to soften and your mind to settle.

Ask, *"What is my soul wanting me to know right now?"*

Then, listen—not with your mind, but with the quiet knowing in your heart. Trust the first gentle nudge you feel even if it is small.

Know that the wisdom you seek is already within you, waiting in the stillness to be heard and remembered.

Write your insight into a journal and let your actions flow from that inner truth.

BUFFY JOHANSON

Buffy Johanson was born and raised in the majestic mountains of Northern Utah. Growing up, she spent her childhood exploring the nearby mountains, reservoirs, and rivers. Answering the call of the wild, she has built a life grounded in her profound love for the natural world and all its creatures, a devotion that extends to her cherished furry companions. The enchanted forest, the sky, and waters of the world provide an infinite source of inspiration for her artwork, creativity, and colorful imagination.

One word that best describes Buffy is curious. With degrees in both Psychology and Social Work from Weber State University and an MBA, she is fascinated with the topics of consciousness, healing, and behavior. Other interests include interior design, architecture, travel, history, and astrology. An adventurer at heart, Buffy is a true wildflower.

Website: www.enchantiful.com

Remembrance:
I Am a Temple of Light

In silence, I journeyed inward and found pathways to healing trauma, letting go of the past, freeing myself of programming and conditioning through remembering who I am.

by Buffy Johanson

My journey of awakening and remembering who I truly am is the path I currently walk. These moments are marked with a broad range of experiences from noteworthy events to simple observations that evoked a-ha moments and all the silent spaces in between. Many of these moments came to me through the thoughtful observations made by colleagues, family, friends, and mentors. A simple question, a comment, an observation; however, I was not prepared for the impact that the power of their words would have on me nor the implications this would have on the trajectory of my life. I knew each of these moments; I could feel their significance vibrating in my body by the strength of my emotional response—tears would instantaneously begin running down my cheeks. Something deep inside was stirring, whispering to me, asking me to look inside myself for answers, to let go of the past, to sit in silence, in presence, to breathe with intention, to be coherent, to listen and to observe without attachment or judgement…to remember. The foundation of who I thought I was and what I knew and understood my life to be…crumbled.

My awakening began with two life-altering events that brought about an incredibly sad time in my life. The passing of my mom in 2019 and my dad in 2022. I loved my parents dearly and talked to them every day, however, these were complicated relationships. I had always felt the weight of family burdens—responsible for others, their feelings and well-being. I was a fixer, but that also came at a price. I was asked to make decisions and take on responsibilities that far outweighed my years. In many ways, I felt at times like the parent, the truth speaker, the easy target, and the scapegoat. As a child, I always felt different, that my world was too small. I was independent, outspoken, always marching to the beat of my own drum, knowing what was right for me—even more than my parents did.

So great was my need for approval and acknowledgement, especially from my mom, that anything other than continually seeking it my entire life was not an option—my self-worth depended on it. I became a perfectionist, hoping this would garner the approval I so craved…it didn't, but the perfectionism stuck. *There must be something wrong with me*, I thought. As I strived every day to be the "perfect" child I felt crazy, because in what world did this make sense? Perfectionism was a mask I chose to wear for an extraordinarily long time. It painted everything in my life with a coat of fear, doubt, comparison, insecurity, and unworthiness. I now understand that none of this was ever about me, but the damage had been done. My mom's passing brought my tireless pursuit to an end without resolution, leaving a painful wound.

It was during the planning of my mom's funeral that I had the first and only heartfelt conversation I ever had with my dad. In a quiet moment in the kitchen he said, "I have always admired you and your ability to stand up for yourself and others. No matter who it is, you don't care. Knowing there will be consequences, you do it anyway. You've been that way your entire life. I wish I could have been more like you. I know at times that was hard for your mom, but she did love you." Powerful words from a man who rarely, if ever, spoke such things and by nature, a peacekeeper at all costs. My heart leapt from my chest and tears instantly filled my eyes and ran down my cheeks. I gave him the biggest hug and told him how much I deeply appreciated his words and him for saying them. I finished with, "I love you, Dad!" I cherish these words, and during one of the saddest days of my life, there was a silver lining—I had been seen.

I was still deep in grief when the world changed, and the second life-altering event happened in my life. Almost a year after my mom's passing, COVID hit. The world turned upside down and I lost all awareness of time. Even as I look back now, this time is still a blur and flew by quickly. Sadly, in 2022, my dad passed away. I was once again swallowed with grief and all the details that came with the finality of wrapping up my parents' lives. Their home had been a constant my entire life, designed and built by my dad, a place I knew I could always go back to if I needed it. Because of this stability, my bohemian spirit never knew fear from taking chances, constantly moving to various places, and following my heart. I was a wanderer and an adventurer with a safety net. With them gone, I was completely untethered from this security for the first time in my life. Although I am a middle-aged adult, it shook me to my core. Another year would pass before I began to move forward again in a meaningful way. In 2023, a completely unexpected gift came into my life. That gift was heart coherence.

Heart coherence had arrived at the perfect time as the lifeline I desperately needed. The events of life had piled up. I was juggling a lot and just trying to hold everything together—including myself. However, I was beginning to fall apart, occasionally breaking out in hives as a stress response to the pressure and anxiety I was carrying. As part of a workshop, the HeartMath® Quick Coherence® Technique was introduced which taught me about heart-focused breathing, activating, and anchoring a positive emotion and coherence. This was life-changing! Over time and with practice, I became centered, clear, calm, my voice was no longer high pitched from stress. I wasn't reactive, and I was able to show up and have conversations in a new and coherent way of which I previously wasn't capable. I also began meditating for the first time in my life. It was during the exploration of different meditations that I rediscovered my love of energy, frequency, vibration, and sound. In this new reality of coherence, doors opened unexpectedly, and I was excited to move through them and explore. My awakening had begun, and I was in uncharted territory.

Ironically, it was once again the words of my dad, one year after his own passing, during a session with a colleague in a mediumship course, which would profoundly devastate me and provide the spark that began my deep dive of reviewing my life and the past. His words were the following: "In order for me to be at peace, I need you to forgive your mother."

The old wound instantly reopened and all the pain and hurt I'd buried with my mom returned with a vengeance. The emotional dam I built had been breached, and all the water came roaring out. There was no stopping it. I was absolutely devastated, instantly crushed, and deeply wounded by his words as tears began rolling down my face. I knew it in my body. It was another a-ha moment. There was something significant about his words, but at the time, I felt so blind-sided and completely thrown off-kilter, because things had been left unresolved. The words had hit a nerve on all the things that I had deeply covered with layers and layers throughout my life, especially where my mom was concerned.

I concealed unworthiness, hurt, anger, disappointment, resentment, longing, sadness, and the confusion of love through the lens of her co-dependency. It was something I did not understand, nor was it anything to which I could relate. My feeling different, misunderstood and not belonging was born from this confusion. Along with guilt and shame, I was still carrying hurt and anger over things she had said, over the occasional looks of anger directed only at me from out of nowhere and for no apparent reason, actions both my parents had taken, that wounded me deeply, and over my mom's unwillingness to ever acknowledge anything I did—even for her or on her behalf. For the next couple of days, my dad's words continued to play over and over again in my head. I was still upset, not yet ready to forgive her, and at the same time, realizing all of this was only hurting me. It was time to revisit the relationship with my mom.

After allowing the initial anger and hurt to subside, I began examining and feeling through this relationship, and what forgiveness and healing would look like. I decided to write her a letter saying all the things left unsaid between us from my point of view. While I wrote, all the traumatic events I had buried for decades came pouring onto the pages. This was a liberating experience, but completely, physically and emotionally, draining. I wasn't sure I had any tears left by the time I finished—I was exhausted. Towards the end, when the wave of emotion had subsided a bit, clarity began to return. I was able to start seeing her, and all she'd lived through, especially the trauma of her childhood. She'd done the best she could and was an amazing mom who lived for and only wanted the best for her children— all the things she never had.

I kept the letter I'd written for a couple of days to give myself time to process and ensure I'd said everything I needed to, and then released it to the fire. This release finally brought peace to this relationship and in forgiving her, I also forgave myself. I always loved my mom and at times my compassion for her was distorted by my own hurt and disappointment. In this moment, I felt complete love and renewed compassion for her, but now a new and vital thread had been woven into the fabric of our story…forgiveness. I love you, Mom, and I forgive you.

Eventually, my mom and her bright, sunny, cheerfulness returned to my life—a true blessing. Despite wanting to take some time off to process everything, I was still surrounded by dense heaviness that I did not understand, nor could I explain it. The past was calling once again; it wasn't going to let me out of its grasp. What was I missing? What lessons hadn't I learned? What was life trying to tell me?

I once again began to feel my way through the past. Heart Coherence had put me back in touch with feelings and they were all coming to the surface after decades of disconnection. I was not always prepared to face or process all the emotions that came my way. I took baby steps as this part of me reawakened from a very long sleep. At this time, all that kept surfacing was hurt, pain, trauma, profound sadness, and shame. It all felt like mine, feelings I had been carrying for as long as I could remember, but like many things, it was something painful that I had always felt, but never questioned, and kept buried deep inside and out of my awareness. I began to ask, "Where was all of this coming from?"

I refer to this time as the "Summer of Healing and Fog" as it was a very confusing chapter in my life. I was trying different healing meditations and healing modalities to help understand, alleviate, and heal all that I was feeling. Nothing much helped and this heaviness was with me constantly and stronger than ever. I was living in and searching through dense fog that would not lift. None of this made sense as I could tie little of what I was feeling back to any event or memory in my past. I was getting frustrated, and my patience was running thin. Without any results to speak of or specifics to go on, I reached out to a friend and mentor and asked if she had time to talk.

I was so excited when Willow agreed to meet. I knew she would bring clarity, and I also valued that she would give me the unfiltered truth—something I love about her and am grateful for. I told her all that was going on in my life. I was talking about responsibilities my parents had always instilled in me since I was a child—instructions on when they passed, what my role would be. When I finished, Willow said, "Did you ever consider that none of this is your responsibility at all, but theirs? That that was their job, not yours." I sat in silence. I couldn't speak, as my mind started to race. What would be the implication if that were true? To be honest, the thought never crossed my mind. I had heard it repeatedly throughout my entire life. Tears began rolling down my cheeks—another significant moment. Despite the tears, I felt lighter, like a weight had been lifted off my shoulders. My curiosity was ignited along with a small, fleeting flicker of anger. I began to wonder, what else had I taken on without question, without awareness? What beliefs did I hold and were they even mine? Could the dense fog and heaviness around me be part of this new discovery? This was my starting point.

It was with this new revelation, my perspective changed completely. I was no longer looking for all the answers in my past, but keys and clues were there in the past of those around me. It was while I was out walking in the woods on a trail by my house that it came to me: all this dense fog of heaviness and emotions was not mine at all, but my mom's.

A memory came to mind when I was in first grade—one that had not been lost to time. I remember my mom dropping me off at school and I started to cry. This had never happened before, because I enjoyed school. Sobbing, I wouldn't get out of the car, telling her how much I loved her and wanted to protect her. Taken aback, most likely as caught off guard as I was by my outburst, she pleaded with me to stop crying. My face was red and blotchy, and I was still slightly trembling from crying. She was able to calm me enough, then she said to take a few more deep breaths, that she loved me and that I was to go into the bathroom, throw cold water on my face, and she would be there to pick me up when school was over. I did as I was told. The same thing happened again for a couple more days, and then never again. It ended as quickly as it began. I was six years old. What did I know of taking on others' emotions, of being energy sensitive, or of being an empath? Of course, this was the dense heaviness that had always been with me, that I had taken on as my own, kept hidden, that was never mine, but had now resurfaced again.

My mom carried with her the trauma of childhood abuse,

alcoholism, and the suicide of her father. A past she rarely, if ever, spoke of, so profound the trauma, it was unthinkable for her to relive or share with anyone. Further complicating matters, her mom, my grandma, lived with us my entire life, and even long before I was born as my mom was her only daughter. The tension and animosity of their relationship lived just under the surface, but never a word was spoken about it. This was not a subject that could or would ever be broached. I felt a lot of guilt because I was very close to and loved my grandma. I worried as a child this relationship might be hurtful to my mom, and I always wondered if this played a part in her and my relationship. This is a question for which I do not have an answer. All of this had happened when I was so young, so impressionable, that I never thought to question any of it. These feelings had always been part of who I thought I was, my identity—broken and unworthy. I now understand these were generational trauma patterns playing out that needed to be healed. I realized I had been ensnared in a web, in a system that I was only beginning to understand.

I was a seeker and had always searched for answers outside of myself, thinking others held the keys to locked doors, to wisdom, to the knowledge and answers I was looking for whether it be in classes, workshops, books, etc. The guidance this time was different, and the message was clear: *You have nothing to learn, no new skills to acquire, only to remember who you are. The answers are within.*

I wasn't sure what I would discover but I listened to the guidance and followed it. The journey inward did not begin with a loud bang but in silence. I began meditating every day by breathing with intention, with presence, coherence, all the while observing without judgment and attachment whatever came up. It only took a few days of being in silence to quickly realize how noisy my everyday life had become and how filled it was with the ease and convenience of technological distractions. I made the decision to minimize the amount of time I spent on these devices.

Over time and as my life quieted down, a routine of daily sacred rituals fell into place that nourished me with expansion and compassion, instead of the exhaustion and disconnection I had become accustomed to. It was the structure I needed. I spent a lot of time in silence, in solitude, and in nature—becoming acutely aware that everything was movement, energy, vibration, sound and frequency. What began as a curious investigation into what was preventing me from remembering and living in this natural state of being who I truly am, became the shock wave that caused my world, my identity, as I knew and understood them, to shatter like glass.

I soon discovered I was living in a vibrational prison, and this was no accident. From the time I was born, the world and those around me started to define me, to determine the framework of who I was. I was given a name, a mask, a costume, the roles I would play, limiting beliefs and traumas that would keep me feeling broken, unworthy and most of all…controllable. All of these components were installed as integrated parts of my programmed identity. From this moment, the misidentification of who I am began. A power structure and system of controls—social, institutional, governmental, religious, past lives and ancestral conditioning— became subtle layers of illusions, lies, and fears that were taught, inherited and part of the collective consciousness that became the foundation of who I thought I was which were constrictive in nature and not expansive. Through this process of programming a false identity, a false self was born. All of these layers, further disconnecting me from who I truly am, shattered fragments out of vibrational alignment, distorting the signal of the light within with layers upon layers of trauma, programming, and conditioning.

The fast pace of today's modern world, technological advances, instant gratification, noise, comforts, distractions, gadgets and all of my experiences and ancestral trauma were traps of control, keeping me busy, looking for answers outside of me, but most of all, distracted and not questioning any of this. All the while, the prison I inhabited, further fortified by my own ignorance and unknowing participation, was designed to keep my life running on an endless replay loop of patterns and cycles. With this new understanding that the vibrational prison was a consequence of what I had learned, been taught, inherited, conditioned, programmed, and reinforced to believe about myself and my reality, the dismantling and my de-identification began.

Silence and inner solitude felt comforting, like I was home. However, quieting my mind in the beginning was the most challenging part of this process as my subconscious, ego, conditioning, and programming wanted to pull me back into the survival mode of fear, previous ways of thinking, believing, and behaving—to old patterns, old loops, old belief systems and old frequencies. For them, change was not an option, and they were not going to make this easy. However, when this happened, I would breathe with intention, refocus, always keeping my awareness in the present moment. A few fundamental truths emerged that served as my foundational pillars as this journey began. First, I am not broken. Second, I did not need to be fixed. Lastly, I was the destination I was always looking for. I was moving through this process without a plan, trusting a steppingstone would be under foot as I took that next step. I surrendered to removing layers and layers of conditioning, limiting beliefs and traumas that formed the bars of my vibrational prison.

There was no more hiding. It was a time of brutal honesty, introspection and observation which was extremely challenging as I had become accustomed to life in this vibrational cage. Even though I had kept things hidden and buried, my vibrational field did not forget the conditioned programming of limitations and fear that was operating most of the time out of my awareness, controlling every aspect of my life, health, and reality. Thoughts and emotions I had never dared to allow myself to think, or even whisper, were faced for the first time. Being completely honest with myself about everything in my life was one of the scariest things I've ever had to do, as this reckoning required absolute vulnerability, non-judgement, self-love and all the courage I could muster. Was I opening Pandora's box? It didn't matter; it was too late. I had new knowledge and understanding; I knew this path was a higher calling to be of service to something greater than myself and, in the core of my being, I knew I could never go back to sleep from this point onward.

Rooted in shame, guilt, fear, etc., memories of my past were regular reminders, never far from a thought or two away depending on the trigger, keeping me trapped and stuck, now wanting to be seen and acknowledged. At first, I sat in silence as many times I couldn't utter a word, but I would patiently wait, tears rolling down my cheeks, until the locks on my secrets and voice released to faint and trembling words. As I spoke aloud to myself in a quiet sacred space, about the past that haunted me, the specific events, choices I had made, and the emotions tied to them, I was no longer the keeper of secrets. Additional forgotten memories bubbled up at various times as a random thought from out of nowhere like a volcanic eruption, a burst of hot lava that caused an instant burn. If I could not speak to something in the moment of recollection, I pinned it. It then became part of that day's or night's rituals. I no longer needed to be perfect, perform, pretend, or appear fine anymore, just be me, and stand in my truth and light. The stratifications I had worn like armor started to slowly peel away, lightening up my world as glimpses of joy returned to my daily life. But something happened then that I did not intend and perhaps naively didn't see coming.

My body began to scream.

The pain, a signal from the depths of my being, was my body saying there is something that wants to be acknowledged. It was energy that had been blocked from decades of repressed and unprocessed experiences and emotional baggage, disconnection, and inherited ancestral trauma. It was excruciating, especially in my lower back and hips. From the moment the trauma occurred, the nervous system caused energy to freeze, crystallize, be stored and stuck in my body, in the fascia and in my vibrational field— the hidden architecture of my patterns. The physical pain had my undivided attention and for the first time in my life, I felt the full weight of all I had buried and been carrying up until this moment. These patterns that once kept me safe, silenced my truth, my body holding what my mind could not, now felt suffocating. I was guided to the ancient wisdom of Somatic Transformation—a process through which I could heal the stories and dissolve old pain, even the pain and stories that did not belong to me, that were being carried in my tissues and body, that I no longer needed to live.

The practice taught me to deeply listen to my body, reclaim it, and move it back into natural alignment. To understand that every part of the body carries meaning and that my pain was not punishment but a portal, the voice of transformation. Healing was about becoming real and began with sound, breath, and vibration. I breathed into those things that once frightened me, staying present through the pain, this choice, helping to rewrite the code and reprogramming my nervous system as it was keeping my body in survival mode. By releasing this energy from a defensive posture through surrender, I returned to a state of safety, becoming a channel of radiance, creativity, openness, creation, and manifestation. Over time, the pain in my body and the bars of my vibrational prison disintegrated and disappeared as one by one my body released the old stories and all that hurt me, now a part of my wisdom. In combination with this practice, additional self-care was also woven into this tapestry of remembering.

I let my intuition and body be my guides. A candle lit, a bath with Epsom salts drawn, to utilize aromatherapy and the healing and soothing properties of water, salt, and candlelight. For harmony and balance, I played music that was upbeat and encouraged me to lighten up, connect with my inner child, be creative and not take things so seriously. Spending time in nature provided support, comfort, and immense strength as love was everywhere I looked. Meditations of sound, vibration, and instrumentation included a wide range of frequencies. It was at this time that I most depended on my body to tell me what it needed. I was patient with myself as it sometimes took a few tries to find the right one, but I would instantly know when my crystalline body sang back…my own built-in tuning fork. It had been several years earlier that the words of my dad cracked me open, just enough for my light to begin to shine through, illuminating this path.

The past and my relationship with my parents, especially my mom, have taken me through the proverbial valley lowlands, strolling through a beloved garden, frozen in the icy tundra, diving the ocean depths, and summiting the highest mountain, all shaping me and leading me to the path I currently walk of remembering who I am. I see my story and my parents very differently now. What if everything I went through with my family, all the proverbial landscapes, was a necessary step to cultivate who I needed to become? An intensive training ground of firsts: challenges, identity, conflicts, triggers, tests, traumas, all designed to develop very specific skills and skillset activations, gifts, resilience and learned experiences. Perhaps the process of growing up was a dress rehearsal for my mission, my purpose, and what I came to do in the world. I love my parents dearly and it is our shared experiences and their words and actions that ignited my paths of awakening and remembering for which I am forever grateful. These family patterns are no longer burdens but a portal for my expansion.

My journey unfolded without a plan as I felt my way through and relied on faith in my internal compass, my heart, which knew my true north; the silence kept me focused inward towards remembrance. Thus, creating space, openness, the fertile soil for seeds of possibility to bloom—ideas, light, creativity, and transformation; all watered with curiosity, wonder and love. In the process, I freed and healed myself and my body from trauma, the vibrational prison I was living in, the matrix of programming, conditioning, and control along with my false identity. My greatest teachers were Ancient Egypt and nature. I combined their guidance, wisdom, knowledge, sacred geometry, codes, and symbols, mirroring the frequency pyramids and tree within. The base and roots, a solid foundation anchored to Mother Earth that would not waver in the midst of chaos. The face and trunk, the light bridge between worlds, and the apex and branches, rising upward toward the sky as I too reach for the light and stars. To align with resonance as an antenna, a receiver, a transmitter of energy, frequency, vibration, sound, and light while anchoring peace, clarity, interconnectedness, and reverence for all things with unconditional love. No longer hidden, no longer silent, and through my expansion, sovereignty, gratitude, and remembrance, I am the Temple of Light I was always meant to be.

My Affirmation

The water remembers and, like water, I flow with the currents of life and follow where they lead; embracing change and easily moving through obstacles, resistance, and fear; finding, trust, clarity, transformation, and unconditional love.

Your Elevation

When we journey inward, the answers are there waiting for us to remember who we truly are. I offer the following invitations:

- Deep breathing with conscious intention to clear the mind and calm the waters of the body. Begin with 5-10 minutes three times per day—a.m., mid-day, and p.m. which offer points of reconnection and reset by placing a hand over your heart center, inhaling, and exhaling with presence, cultivating, and feeling gratitude.

- Spend time in silence (start with 10 minutes) as a daily time of connection by listening, feeling, and receiving, acknowledging whatever arises.

- Be in nature and deeply listen and feel its music, its sounds. Take a 20-minute daily walk in the park or on the beach, go barefoot on the earth, or sit amongst the trees.

Elevate Your Life

You have incredible power within you—an innate ability to completely transform your life. What has happened to you matters. The challenges you are navigating are very real—they are a part of your story and your growth. But none of this defines your future. You possess the ability to rise above it all, to heal, and to create a new path forward, one rooted in your true essence and limitless potential. You can consciously design the life you desire from a place of wholeness and elevated resilience.

Since the universe is always listening and responding to the energy you put out—through your thoughts, your words, your emotions, and your actions—you have the power to influence your path simply by being mindful. It's about paying close attention to what you're thinking, how you're speaking, and how you're engaging with your life. When you do that with intention, you start to shape your future deliberately. And the good news is, you don't have to stay where you are. Just a few simple, conscious shifts can completely elevate your experience and invite more joy, abundance, and fulfillment into every part of your life.

Suggested Step #1
Empowering Questions to Ask the Universe

What Are Empowering Questions?

Empowering questions are intentional, open-ended inquiries that invite a deeper connection with the universe's abundant wisdom. When you ask these questions, you're signaling to the universe that you're receptive to guidance, opportunity, and growth beyond your current circumstances. They create an energetic openness, allowing insights, inspired ideas, and unexpected blessings to flow into your life.

Instead of focusing on limitations or what's not working, empowering questions help you to tune in to what could be—recognizing that you are co-creating your reality with the universe. These questions help you soften resistance, expand your awareness, and begin to see beyond transient challenges to the infinite options that can elevate your life.

By consistently asking empowering questions, you send a clear message to the universe: *"I am worthy and open to receiving miracles, a new path, and greater possibilities for my life."*

When Should You Use Empowering Questions?

- **As a Daily Practice:** Set aside a few moments each day—perhaps in the morning or evening—to cultivate a space where positive change and new opportunities naturally emerge.

- **During Moments of Frustration or Difficulty:** Instead of allowing frustration, doubt, or negativity to crash your vibe, become an active co-creator of your experience and open channels for new solutions and divine guidance.

- **When Feeling Stuck or Overwhelmed:** Realign your energy by asking questions to support you in discovering one step you can take toward your highest good or exploring ways to invite more trust and ease into your experience.

- **During Reflection or Meditation:** Use them as prompts to delve deeper into your inner landscape, uncover hidden beliefs, or connect with your higher self. This deepens your relationship with yourself and strengthens your intuitive guidance.

- **As a Tool for Cultivating Possibilities:** Whenever you're seeking inspiration or proactive energy, ask empowering questions. They serve as a catalyst for expanding your awareness and inviting divine opportunities.

1. What opportunities are beginning to present themselves to me right now that I haven't realized?

2. What might I be holding back from allowing myself to receive?

3. What choice or option is available to me in this moment that serves my highest good?

4. What perspectives or new beliefs could elevate my mindset in this moment?

5. What positive qualities am I not seeing in this experience (or person)?

6. Is there a gift or lesson in this situation that I could acknowledge and celebrate?

7. What am I being invited to recognize, shift, or understand about myself through this experience?

8. What lessons am I meant to learn from this experience?

9. Is there something I haven't acknowledged yet that I am being invited to be grateful for in this moment?

10. What actions, strengths or talents am I being called to activate now that will allow the best possible outcome?

11. How could I increase my feelings of joy, peace, and ease today?

12. What beliefs would help me feel more confident, safe, and secure to move forward?

13. What mindset or energy do I need to shift to invite more ease into this situation?

14. What can I do differently to feel lighter and more receptive to joy and abundance?

15. What support or resources might be available to me that I've overlooked or need to tap into?

16. Is there any unspoken truth or feeling I am avoiding that if expressed could lead me to be more connected to my peace?

17. Are there any choices I am avoiding that could help live in greater alignment with my true values and purpose?

18. What options or perspectives am I refusing to consider that could change my experience entirely for the better?

19. How can I bring more spontaneity, fun, or playfulness into my current circumstances?

20. If I believed everything was happening for my highest good, what would I be willing to accept?

Empowering questions like these are simple and easy to incorporate into your daily routine. They don't require special tools or lengthy processes—just a moment of intention and curiosity. Ask these questions from your heart. They will help you feel more grounded, supported, and confident in navigating whatever comes your way—amplifying your ability to navigate life with authentic resilience and a whole lot more grace.

Suggested Step #2
The Ritual of Writing

Why Journal?

Writing allows you to connect deeply with yourself, process emotions, and release what no longer serves you. It creates a sacred space for healing, reflection, and discovering your true essence beyond conditioned beliefs. Journaling is a gentle act of self-love and empowerment—an ongoing practice that helps you nurture your resilience and align with your highest self.

It provides you a safe space to process emotions, release heavy energy, and gain clarity—allowing you to discover more about yourself, from what you believe to your greater truth.

It becomes a gentle container for grief, anger, hope, and joy—enabling these feelings to move through you rather than get stuck. Over time, journaling helps peel back layers built by conditioning, revealing your most authentic self and can empower you to live more consciously.

When to Journal

This is different for everyone. Some find it helpful in the morning to set intentions and connect with their inner wisdom before they start their day. Others prefer the evening, or right before bed to help process what unfolded in their day. You might also choose moments of emotional upheaval, feeling overwhelmed or inspired, when you need a safe space to express your true thoughts. The key is to listen to your needs and choose moments when you can be fully present and available for yourself.

A Sacred Practice

Approach your writing with reverence and mindfulness. Set an intention before each session—perhaps to be honest, gentle, or open-hearted. You might also find it helpful to create a space that feels safe and calming—light a candle, play soft music, or even meditate for a few minutes before starting. This will help you shift into a more peaceful, reflective state.

Write slowly, with intention, knowing that your words hold energy and potential for transformation. When intense emotions arise, remember that it's okay to step away from your writing. Write until you feel expressed, then shred or safely burning them. This clears heavy energies and protects your inner space.

Most importantly, be gentle with yourself—your words are sacred, and the act of writing is a way of honoring your evolving self.

Here are some deep, reflective journal prompts to support your Elevated Resilience journey:

1. What parts of myself am I most afraid to show, and what would it feel like to embrace them fully?

2. What patterns or beliefs have I outgrown, and what new truths are emerging as I evolve?

3. When do I feel most connected to my authentic self, and how can I nurture that connection daily?

4. What emotions do I tend to avoid, and what might they be trying to tell me?

5. How do I define resilience, and how have I demonstrated resilience in my life so far?

6. What does healing mean to me, and what steps can I take to support my healing journey?

7. In what areas of my life do I feel most stuck, and what small actions could help me move forward?

8. What are my deepest desires for myself and my life?

Treat your practice with reverence and you'll uncover new layers of yourself as you journey along your path toward a more empowered, authentic life.

Suggested Step #3
Practice Gratitude

What Is Gratitude?

Gratitude is the heartfelt acknowledgment and appreciation of what you already have—the people, experiences, qualities, and things that bring joy, comfort, and meaning to your life. It is a powerful vibrational state that elevates your energy, shifting it from feelings of lack, frustration, or suckiness to joy, abundance, and more optimism. When you practice gratitude, you align yourself with a positive frequency that attracts even more of what you desire for your life.

Why It Matters

The energy of gratitude has the greatest potential to create meaningful shifts—not just in your mood, but in your life circumstances. When you focus on what you're thankful for, you raise your vibration, which opens the door to new opportunities, improved relationships, and a deeper sense of fulfillment.

But gratitude is powerful for more than just shifting your mindset. It is about tapping into the emotional energy behind your appreciation. Genuine gratitude involves feeling truly thankful and emotionally connected to the blessings in your life. This deep emotional resonance amplifies the energetic shift needed to attract the changes you crave for your life.

When you connect emotionally with what you are grateful for, you activate a vibrational frequency that can accelerate powerful, meaningful shifts. The energy of your emotion, when paired with the frequency of gratitude, not only transforms your perspective from one of scarcity to one of abundance, but it also creates a magnetic energetic field that attracts more of what you desire, amplifying your ability to manifest and thrive.

Amp Up the Gratitude

Your words carry power. Speak and write as if your dreams are already fulfilled—because in the realm of energy and manifestation, they are.

- **Make a gratitude list:** Write down at least ten things you're grateful for each day. Feel the appreciation as you list them—this helps anchor positive energy.

- **Rampage your gratitude:** Take 3 minutes to speak out loud in a gratitude rampage—shout, sing, dance about as you recite all the things you're thankful for.

- **Gratitude for manifesting:** Write intentions for your life as if what you desire has already manifested— 'as if' you are living your ideal life now. For example, *"I am so happy and grateful now that [insert desire]."*

The more you cultivate gratitude, the more your vibration rises, opening the doors to greater opportunities, happiness, and fulfillment. And with a gratitude journal you never have to worry about someone reading it—let them! If anything, it will inspire them towards living an elevated life too!

Unveil Your Voice—Embrace Your Story. Transform Your Life.

Are you ready to share your story?

Whether you see yourself as an author or simply have a powerful message to share, this journey is for you. If your goal is to support, inspire, and create positive change, **The Writer from Within, Elevated** is a collaborative publishing experience designed to guide you every step of the way.

Break through barriers, be supported, and see your story come to life—**your story is a vital spark in a universe of limitless potential.**

Visit: bonniewirth.ca/writer-from-within

Testimonials for the
Writer from Within Program

This program is oozing with structured guidance, support, experience, and wisdom that places you on a safe path to write your story with confidence and authenticity. Bonnie serves as an inspiration, source of enlightenment, encourager, and cheerleader, guiding you throughout the process of sharing your story in the most authentic and aligned manner within your truth. Additionally, the community of writers that gathers is an added benefit. If you feel compelled to share your story and require assistance in its publication that includes meticulous care, attention and utmost integrity, I encourage you to consider enrolling in Bonnie's program, Writer From Within.

–Marianne Lipsius

———•·•———

Writer From Within is a transformational experience on so many levels. The writing itself—with a guaranteed publication—led me to a time in my life I thought I had handled, but there was so much more to express, and heal. The process, led by Bonnie Wirth, was an unconditionally loving and supportive space, without which I could never have gone into the depths that I traveled. Challenging and rewarding, it is without hesitation and with great enthusiasm, that I recommend both the Writer From Within program and Bonnie Wirth.

–Patricia Scott

———————•◦•———————

Participating in the Writer From Within program has been an extraordinary experience. The guidance, encouragement, and heartfelt support helped me bring my story to life while also nurturing healing and self-discovery. Through this process, I learned to trust my voice, honor my truth, and express it with authenticity. It has reinforced for me the power and importance of sharing our stories. I am deeply grateful for the opportunity to be part of such an inspiring and transformative program.

–Brenda Gerling

———————•◦•———————

Bonnie Wirth believed in me as an author long before I believed in myself. I joined her Writer From Within class with much reservation; however, with her gift for making her students feel safe and supported I was excited to join her weekly group. Her ability to provide a safe and supportive environment made sharing our stories a very powerful and healing journey. Her enthusiasm for writing is so contagious I'm looking forward to seeing what's next.

–Cathy Morrison

———————•◦•———————

I recommend the Writer from Within program to anyone who wants to dig deep into getting to know oneself all within a safe space made up of kind mentors and inspiring women who are equally resilient. The end result, in having all of our deeply personal stories side by side in one published volume, is also a dream come true.

–Carolyn Hampton

Writer from Within truly helped me find comfort in writing. From Bonnie and the guest authors, I learned writing strategies and tools and found courage to trust the words that are in me. From this amazing group of women, I found immeasurable support and created a sisterhood and shared vision...I've added to my tribe! I have experienced something far greater than me...something that I can take into my future writing—Confidence!

–Rita Herperger

To say that a chapter in a book will change your life would be an understatement. The writer from within program by Bonnie Wirth really does take you within. It is an enrichment of your inner and outer world; a shift that changes you and those around you. You and your soul wouldn't want to miss out on this safe space to expand and grow.

–Lori Burris

Writer From Within has been a life-changing experience. I had always dreamed of writing my story, and this program gave me the courage to begin. Bonnie's unwavering encouragement and sensitivity to Spirit guided me through moments of fear and doubt. The greatest gift was becoming part of a beautiful, supportive community of like-minded women. The wisdom shared by published authors and Bonnie's genuine love for each participant created an environment of healing, growth, and joy. This journey not only helped me write—it helped me understand myself and others more deeply.

–Mary Driver

Participating in the Writer-from-Within was an incredibly cathartic experience! I don't consider myself a writer, joining was simply a prompt from my guides that I agreed to follow. Even before the program began, fear crept in and made me question my decision, but once I met the group with Bonnie and Michael, I felt welcomed and watched my fear calmly take a seat beside me. Though the process was metaphorically excavating with fear insistent and firm to take control, the group's heart was as relentless in weaving together the most compassionate and sincere blanket of support which became my vessel to witness the illusory cocoon like quality of fear. The group's caring energy ultimately became the momentum I needed to transform my fear into courage - embodying and letting my writer within to step forward. This program is for anyone who seeks to overcome their fears and unlock new potential within themselves in the process.

–Barrie Tugade

www.ingramcontent.com/pod-product-compliance
Lightning Source LLC
Chambersburg PA
CBHW051303120626
46547CB00015B/2062